CUBA: prophetic island

By the same author

Story

THE UNWELCOME MAN
THE DARK MOTHER
RAHAB
CITY BLOCK
HOLIDAY
CHALK FACE
THE DEATH AND BIRTH OF DAVID MARKAND
THE BRIDEGROOM COMETH
SUMMER NEVER ENDS
ISLAND IN THE ATLANTIC
THE INVADERS
NOT HEAVEN

History

OUR AMERICA
VIRGIN SPAIN
THE REDISCOVERY OF AMERICA
AMERICA HISPANA: A PORTRAIT AND
  A PROSPECT
DAWN IN RUSSIA
CHART FOR ROUGH WATER
SOUTH AMERICAN JOURNEY
BIRTH OF A WORLD: BOLIVAR IN TERMS
  OF HIS PEOPLES
BRIDGEHEAD: THE DRAMA OF ISRAEL
THE REDISCOVERY OF MAN
CUBA: PROPHETIC ISLAND

Essay

SALVOS
TIME-EXPOSURES (BY "SEARCHLIGHT")
IN THE AMERICAN JUNGLE
USTEDES Y NOSOTROS (IN SPANISH ONLY)
THE JEW IN OUR DAY
PRIMER MENSAJE A LA AMERICA HISPANA (IN SPANISH ONLY)

Theater

NEW YEARS EVE

CUBA:

prophetic island

Waldo Frank

Marzani & Munsell, INC. *Publishers, New York, N.Y.*

Copyright © 1961 by Waldo Frank

All rights reserved. No part of this book in
excess of five hundred words may be reproduced
in any form without permission in writing
from the publisher.

Printed in the United States of America

A Personal Foreword

In 1959, the first year of Castro's government in Havana, I was asked to visit Cuba. I had known it under both Batista and Machado. Armando Hart Davalos, the minister of education, seconded by Chancellor Raul Roa as chairman of the office of cultural relations, invited me to write a book on Cuba. The younger generation, now in command, had read my books and believed that I understood America and America Hispana. Many of the older generation, frequently imprisoned or exiled by dictators, had read my clandestine letters to the university students. President Dorticos had said to Hart: "There should be a Waldo Frank portrait of Cuba." What they wanted was a work, in their own words, "to stand beside such books as *Birth of a World*: Bolivar in terms of his peoples; *America Hispana*: a portrait and a prospect; and *Virgin Spain*. The invitation, of course, would not have come, if my past work had not revealed *simpatia* and what to them seemed comprehension of America Hispana. But there was never the slightest inquiry as to what the book would say, what it would *be*. The grant I received enabled me to devote the two years I needed for my task: to research, travel, study and writing. And of course my single obligation was to the truth: to seek and to express the truth as I found it.

When, in 1959, I accepted the task, there was already trouble between Cuba and the State Department. But the situation was not hopeless. Cuba had confidence in America; we all had confidence that the whole truth of Cuba would be told and would be heard. Pathetically symbolic were the posters all over Havana welcoming a congress of travel agents and inviting them to see for themselves the peace and joy of the revolution.

No one would have predicted *an invasion!* No one was ready to believe in the deterioration of continent and hemisphere relations that less than three years have wrought.

The extent to which the sin and the responsibility for this go to the U.S.A.: to the fears of the American economic system, above all to the ignorance of virtually all American officials on the realities of Cuba and America Hispana, the reader is in a position to decide for himself. Upon the objectivity of his judgment will depend the chance of a renewal of good relations. This is certain: Cuba at present stands for America Hispana. Individual governments among the Hispanic republics may "side" with the U.S., because of fear of American ill-will, because of economic pressure, because American Capitalism has many friends in places of power. Let no one be fooled by this. The Hispanic *peoples* respond to our conduct in Cuba as if their own bodies were touched and offended. And soon or late, the *peoples* will be heard, even if this means the repudiation of their most consequential leaders.

Therefore it is extremely fortunate, not only for Cuba but for America Hispana *and for the United States,* that our stupid and criminal attempt to invade Cuba was a fiasco.

There is still time for us Americans to learn that such an invasion of counter-revolution as the one we engineered is an attack on all our deepest values *at home, here,* in the United States. There is still time for us Americans to learn that much of what we call "the crimes" of Communism is simply the universal psychology of war; and that it reigns and spreads in the United States no less than in Russia and in Cuba; and that the way to save the United States and Cuba is not to feed and foment the psychology of war (which we then self-righteously lament as "Communism") but to return to a psychology of peace by replacing the aims of peace for the present bombs and embargoes.

W. F.

Contents

Prelude
The United Nations and the Heat of Cuba

THE United Nations is surrounded by New York: old and dirty
streets of slum that will soon be torn down, shops, factories
and the East River fetid with chemical waste and sewage.
Within these survivals of the nineteenth century age of coal,
the gleaming United Nations buildings flaunt prophecy of a
new world—and a warning. For the floor after floor of great
glass façades, the stairs prancing like the flying buttresses of a
cathedral, the walls white or clad in tapestry and mural—
these seem fragile, vulnerable to the oily smoke falling from
high industrial chimneys. Could the old murky brick have a
longer life than the United Nations buildings—longer than
their abstract geometry of space, brittle as glass; than their
air-conditioned halls; than the delegates' lounge whose stuffed
furniture might so easily be reduced to rubble?

The great General Assembly auditorium is a truncated pyra-
mid of colors. The walls—gold, black-ribbed—are immense
half-opened fans, faintly a-sway in the airs of the orations.
The two rostrums, one above the other, one for the Assembly
officers and one for the speaker, suggest marble, bluish and
aquamarine. But the cluttered delegates' tables, yellow and
blue; the part-red, part-cerulean walls with abstract paintings;
the cubicles for press and television; the balconies for the
tourists—all combine to suggest a flamboyant dahlia. And a
flower, however huge, is fragile. And the fragile is fleeting.

The Assembly Hall's flower effect brings coolness. The lounge
and bar are cool. The six women telephone operators near the
bar call the delegates with cool voices. The coolness of these

ladies and of the lounge around them sustains the impression of fragility, the impression of a country club poised tenuously over the heat of the world's teeming squalor.

The membership of this ecumenical country club has expanded and changed within the decade. There are more dark faces (a quarter of all the nations are African), more turbans and more graciously flowing robes. But the civilian uniform of Western diplomacy and bureaucracy still rules. The delegates from Europe (which is the mere western nub of Eurasia), the delegates from the Americas (a minority hemisphere) and from the United States (soon to be in size, population and potential power a minority nation in the minority hemisphere) yet register the tone and the temperature of coolness. Even the men whose faces are black speak impeccably the French of Paris or the English of Oxford and continue the coolness of their recent masters. Over a seething earth of human hungers —for bread, for freedom and for power—the United Nations hangs suspended in an air of fragile, flimsy coolness.[1]

On September 26, 1960, the president of the Assembly—an Irish gentleman whose hypercourteous, hyperlegal language was not cool but frozen—gave the floor to the president of the Cuban delegation. Fidel Castro stepped forward to the rostrum.

His first words were: "Although it has been said of us that we speak at great length, you may be sure that we shall try to be brief, and to put before you only what we consider our duty to say." He spoke for four and a half hours. "We shall also," he went on, "speak slowly in order to cooperate with the interpreters." After ten minutes, his words were so flowing and so flooding that the interpreters could attempt no more than minute digests, snatched as from a torrent. And yet it would be wrong to say he broke his promise. Fidel Castro gave the Assembly a brief history of Cuba and its relations with the

1. The facts of modern man and of the nations compel this critical snapshot of the United Nations. But no less real are man's dire needs and high aims. For all its weaknesses and falsities, it would be catastrophic for the United Nations to cease to exist.

government of the United States through a century and a half. Nothing less could have communicated his point to a body of men and women overwhelmingly ignorant of Cuba. And for that purpose, four and a half hours were not long enough. But to the Assembly delegates and the world most of them represent, these hours were long indeed. As for his promise to speak "slowly": the word is relative. And for years now this man has been speaking to Cubans: on television, on public squares of villages and cities, in the cooperatives and the new schools, in remote mountain farms and all the night through at home to his colleagues—spelling out Cuba's economic and political problems in great detail, at a speed which, by contrast, made his address to the United Nations seem tortoise-slow.

Many—probably most—of the delegates were sympathetic with what Castro was saying about the past sufferings of the Cuban people. A number approved what he and his people were doing and had achieved in Cuba. Probably all, except the United States delegates, enjoyed (if only *sub rosa*) his volley of facts from the time of John Quincy Adams and Henry Clay to the present—facts revealing the possessiveness and the aggressiveness of American government policy toward Cuba and its indifference to the aspirations of the Cuban people. But practically all—even most of the delegates from the other Hispano-American nations—disapproved in one or another form the man's methods in word and in deed, although they approved Cuba's aim of independence. The Russians, of course, were having a good time. But Khrushchev's temperature, like a good actor's, was cool. There was a radical difference of *heat* between the passionate Cuban and the Assembly. And although they listened, more patient than rapt, for four and a half hours, the difference of temperature excluded comfort on both sides: the delegates' and Castro's.

Cuba as a nation was being *born*. What was happening in Cuba since the July 26 Movement of 1953 was not rebirth, not political and economic revolution, but birth. And birth is hot. George Washington knew such heat; it warmed the freezing and the starving at Valley Forge. Bolivar had it, flinging his armies across the icy peaks of the Andes. The chief block to deep communication between Castro and the Assembly was on that day and remains the difference between a heat which effects physical transformation and a coolness which above all else needs to remain what it is, to resist the molecular changes of incandescence.

Whom did the delegates, the press, the American public see, watching Castro's speech? A very tall young man, standing erect in an undecorated, olive-green fatigue uniform. Castro had gone down to Santiago, Chile, to say: "Our revolution is not red but olive-green. One step ahead of both the right and the left, this is a *humanist* revolution, because it does not deprive man of his essence, but holds the *whole man* as its fundamental aim. . . . Capitalism sacrifices the man, the Communist state by its totalitarian concept sacrifices the rights of man. We agree with neither." These words his audience at the United Nations did not hear. They saw a face of strong harmonious features: the nose rising straight without a dip into the forehead, as in a classical Greek statue. They saw a beard of black, suffused with overtones of red wherever sun or the hall's light struck it. They did not see his eyes, hotly defensive as they met the eyes of the Assembly. They saw a body still boyishly fluent, not without heaviness and softness: the body of a sensuous man, needing more exercise than he had time for. ("I often long back to the days of roughing it in the Sierra Maestra.") And when he spoke, they might not understand or concur in what he was saying, but they heard the voice of a strange duality: a voice like a cello, whose basic tones are deep and slow, being played at great speed in the higher registers, competing with the violin.

In these high notes was pleading—and defiance; and in the lower notes an underlying lament for the sufferings of his people, a suffering long in time, often sharp in terror or frozen by the callousness of succeeding masters.

In Cuba, Castro's voice *connects*—whether he is explaining the complexities of sugar prices to a half-dozen workers casually met on a street corner or addressing the country on the air to mourn the defection of an old friend, editor of a magazine, who fears that the Communists are about to devour Cuba.

Here in the Assembly Hall, the rapport is absent. And the untidy beard disturbs the decorous delegates, many of whom wear dapper goatees and Van Dykes. Castro's explanation of how the rebel soldiers in the mountains came to wear beards is simple: "At first we had no razors, so we let our beards grow. Later we made a vow not to shave our beards until Batista was out of the country. Then, there was always so much else to do. . . ." Castro's voice tapers off in reminiscence. Castro thinks of himself as a modern, and the beard, he must know, harks back to the romantic early nineteenth century of Spain. It would not fit the pin-striped American businessman, or the equally compulsive Communist engineer of revolution, or the expert technician who is so sure of a new world built exclusively by science. The beard reveals in Castro and in his movement something of the epoch of romantic revolutions: a utopian spirit, but with painstaking, precise methods, that the utopias never dreamed of. The bearded youth seem to say: "We are the sons of our forefathers."

The Assembly eyes do not see these deep roots. They look at this man in his faded uniform, shrink from his fire and do not understand it. To them, even to those who like him and approve his deeds, he is a figure standing by himself, leveling down all opposition, giving dictatorial orders to his supine people. They know there have been no elections in Cuba. They know that the opposition press, shrinking day by day, its writers threatened by angry printers who refuse to set editorials hostile to the new Cuba, has virtually vanished. "Totalitarian! Communist!" their uncomfortable thoughts conclude, and shape their minds. They do not see that, with at least 80 per cent of the people fervidly for Castro and the whole country in the throes of passionate construction, with no issue thinkable

for them except *Patria o Muerte,* a period for elections would
be a bothersome delay, a pretext for sabotage. A people must
cool down in the surety that it is going to survive before it can
then go to the polls—as the Americans went, a dozen years after
the declaration and the war for independence. And the Assembly delegates do not see that there are times of national
fervor when an opposition press becomes a nuisance. The
great reactionary newspaper *Diario de la Marina,* which abused
Marti and favored Spain throughout the Cuban Thirty Years
War for Independence (1869–1898), could have survived the
scarcity of buyers and the anger of the people only if the
government had paid its debts and protected its linotype machines with soldiers. Such a policy toward reactionary presses
might have been clever of Castro. But he is too direct to be
clever.

A hint of the man's difference from the dictators of Latin
America, of Europe and of Asia—the army men captives of
army values, the power men chained to power—may be
glimpsed in the little group listening to their leader at the Assembly. There is Captain Antonio Nuñez Jimenez, executive
director of INRA,[2] the all-powerful agency for the Agrarian
Reform. His black beard is neater than Castro's, his skin is
gleaming white and his venturous eyes soften their heat with
constant playfulness and humor. Nuñez Jimenez is the chief
speleologist in Cuba, an island of many deep and mysterious
caves. Before joining Castro, he taught geography at the University of Havana. And he has written a huge *Geografia de
Cuba,* which is unique in its inclusion of history and battles as
legitimate aspects of geography. "I am one of the old ones," he
says smiling. "I am thirty-seven!" The synthesis of his devotions
—for his family, for his central task of transmitting Cuba in
viable forms to the Cubans, and for his fossil hunts in caves and
mountain valleys—becomes visible in his resilient body and
quick laughter.

Next to him sits the Cuban Minister for Foreign Relations,

2. Instituto Nacional de la Reforma Agraria.

Raul Roa. Roa (who shaves) began his career as a liberal writer by fighting the dictatorship of Machado. He became dean of the humanities at the University of Havana, and for a generation has been in close touch with the intellectual life of the Americas and Europe. In politics now, he has never lost his academic touch. He is a tense, nervous, slender and rhythmic man whose sensitivities constantly threaten, but never overwhelm, his detachment. In the need of his cause, Cuba's independence, he could be ruthless. His grandfather, a landowning aristocrat and friend of Marti, fought in the war of 1869 against Spain, and Spain's great tradition of rebellion from crown and church is in him, as it was in Bolivar. Indeed, Nuñez Jimenez and Raul Roa, men of distinctly different backgrounds, seem to have a common source in some portrait by El Greco.

A woman of early middle age (perhaps it would be more revealing to say "of mature youth") quietly comes down the aisle to give a message to Chancellor Roa. This is Celia Sanchez, gracious, intelligent and homely, who in the very first months forsook her comfortable bourgeois home in the northeastern port of Nicaro to join the revolution. She has never left it. Before the victory, in the mountains, she was housekeeper and mother to the camp, solving the heavy problems of food, equipment, medicines; easing the clashes of temperament and the headaches of her boys. She has not changed since the victory. If you are in a legitimate hurry to see Castro, the best way is to reach Celia. Castro's life in Cuba is a perpetual journey. He has a home, and almost never sees it. He regrets the need of his constant sallies over all the island, but he enjoys them. Office work is harder for him, and he suspects office perspectives.[3] When he is unbearably fatigued after a long succession of twenty-hour days, he steals away to Celia's small apartment, and she hides him.

While at the United Nations, the Cuban delegation occupied

3. Castro explained to me that he was trying to departmentalize his office work: certain days for certain duties. I doubt if he has managed.

half a floor of the Hotel Theresa, in black Harlem, to avoid
what seemed to Castro the extortion of one New York hotel
and the inhospitality of others. Celia at once took upon herself the task of lessening the chaos within the inadequate
quarters. When Fidel was too busy to eat, she prepared soup
on her electric burner and spooned it into him while he went on
talking.[4]

Exposed up there on his rostrum, Fidel Castro appears *to be*
the Cuban revolution. But this appearance is an oversimplifica-
tion, as it is falsely simple to represent a profound national
and cultural birth as a mere turnover in economics—and as it
is dangerous nonsense to label this deep business "Communist."
Behind Castro are 450 years of Cuban history and a culture
far older than Cuba. Castro and his colleagues are culture
products as well as producing agents of the revolutionary culture. Castro knows this, though he simplifies matters when he
speaks. Every time I have seen him alone, he has spoken to
me of a pet project: the community for writers he wants to
set up on the Isle of Pines. This is as urgent to his intimate
needs as a solution of the problem of sugar monoculture. It
proves that the golden age of Spanish art and letters is not
alien to him: the age when great poets such as St. John of
the Cross, St. Teresa and Luis de Leon were at work in
monasteries.

Castro further simplifies, and distorts, by speaking more of
Cuba's sufferings than of its strengths. Stressing events which
he explains as invasions, exploitations and betrayals of Cuba,
he does not explicitly state the evidence of himself and his fellows that Cuba is a fertile, vibrant, lusty and pre-potent island.
True, as he informs the Assembly, when Batista was thrown
out:

. . . 37.5 per cent of Cubans were illiterate; 70 per cent of
rural Cuban children had no teachers; 2 per cent of our

4. See Appendix 2.

population had tuberculosis . . . 95 per cent of the rural children were suffering from parasites. Infant mortality was astronomical; the standard of living was the reverse. . . . 85 per cent of the small farmers were paying rent on their land that came to a third of their gross income; and 1.5 per cent of all the landowners possessed 46 per cent of the total area of the country.

Castro went on:

Public services, electricity, telephone, etc.—all belonged to or were controlled by United States monopolies. Likewise the banking business, the export-import trade, the sugar and oil refineries, the lion's share of all arable land, most of which lay idle.

True, all true. But no less true that the Cubans today appear to be a happy people.

But what is happiness? We once defined as happy the man whose energies flow unimpeded. Then the addict, completely given to his drug—physical or metaphysical—is happy? The man wholly possessed by rage or passion? The beatnik devoted unreservedly to defeat? The Fascist with his callow egomania serving a *Herrenvolk?* The Communist fanatically certain that he and he alone has the Absolute Truth? We must amend our definition. Call the man happy whose flow of energy is both unimpeded and harmonious with man's true nature and health. Without dogma or conscious philosophy, without delusion, therefore without distortion, the youth of Cuba appear to be happy in their task of creating a country. We shall see. . . . But this is certain: *the energy must be there.* Despite the chronic unemployment . . . the disease . . . of which Castro speaks, the Cuban youth's joy and gaiety in their concentrated duties prove their health of energy. No maimed people could behave as the Cubans are behaving; and even Castro himself is a result of these energies. What will happen next, if and when the relatively simple tasks of possessing the island and making the nation have been accomplished, is another question.

But the Assembly hearer, listening to Castro, could not catch this counterpoint of strength and suffering. Castro spoke of starving Cubans, and was lusty. He spoke of illiterate Cubans and was well read.[5] He spoke of suffering in the voice of a cantor singing the Lamentations of Jeremiah, and was full of high animal spirits. But Castro's energy is not alone in Cuba. Castro was never alone, even when with eleven others (survivors of one hundred) he reached the Sierra Maestra, near Santiago, and declared war on Batista's army of 20,000, trained and equipped by the United States. The abundant land and the land's folk were with him.

Cuba belongs within the culture of America Hispana. Cuba took a long time to learn this. It may indeed be said not to have known this until the mid-nineteenth century, when Jose Antonio Saco was moved to write *Contra la Anexión*, because among cultivated Cubans there were so many who favored annexation to the United States. Cuba did not know this conclusively until Jose Marti, a generation later, wrote his great pamphlets on America and Cuba's place in it, and Cuba's relation with the America of the North.

Despite the intellectual sophistication of the Hispano-American world dreamed of by such poets as Marti, Heredia, and Placido, the Cubans themselves remained an unsophisticated people. Only a folk of innocence would have undertaken the "impossible" tasks of reconstruction outlined in Cuba's laws of agrarian and urban reform, and of industrial and financial nationalization—in the face of the hostile neighbor, the most powerful of nations. When we come to the story of Castro's two initial assaults on Batista's army: the attack on the great barracks in Santiago and the landing from Mexico in a leaky

5. In March 1961, Armando Hart, Minister of Education, proclaimed the immediate cessation of all schools: students and teachers to become temporary "squads to stamp out illiteracy" before December of that year, when—illiteracy gone—regular studies will be resumed.

vessel, innocence will be the word that occurs to us. But not without great shrewdness, not without a precise and expedient timing. (Consider, for example, the swiftness and cunning with which Castro took advantage of the stupidity of the New York hotels by going up to Harlem, thereby winning a good press in all of Africa.)[6]

Bear the paradox in mind, if you would understand the deeds of Castro: deeds directed by studious, detailed knowledge of his people and of all America Hispana, yet released by a basic innocence, an almost childlike innocence that may rush in and act where political maturity would falter.

These deeds have changed the face of Cuba; cleared the thorny and impassable *marabú* that choked the idle acres and turned it into fuel; transformed Batista's barracks into schools and built thousands of new schools; matched cooperative farms with stores and new local industry (even a steel mill is planned). For the first time opened the beaches to the people, put up motels for them; drained swamps; planted rice and cotton, henequen and over a million trees. Above all, made it known that Cubans are a joyous people.

All this has been done, but not without waste, error and superficial chaos that could deepen. The machinery of complex social action must be improvised in the act. But the inward order of an organic birth is there. This, the Assembly hearers do not consciously know.

Yet somehow they sense it, as their fear proves. Castro as the enemy of the malodorous Batista, was popular. Within a few months the press and the liberals, almost without exception, had turned against him. The court-martials of hundreds of war criminals, the narrowing of the Havana press to virtual propaganda and the defection of earlier friends and leaders were played up—although such are, and always have been, concomitants of social change and industrial revolution. Cuba's *people* and what they were trying to do were ignored or mis-

6. See Appendix 2.

represented beyond the scope of ignorance. Why? Instinctively, these opponents knew that more was at stake than reforms long overdue; that a new world was in birth which, if it was not stopped, must destroy not only the American hegemony over Cuba and the hemisphere, but the hegemony of blind forces and false values in the United States. The correspondents who reported about Cuba, *and left out the Cuban people,* were really "defending" the American people from an appraisal of our television-commodity culture—an appraisal of *our* values, that might inspire change of heart and mind at home. For the liberals, above all, make a cult of advocating little changes to prevent big ones. And the changes taking place in Cuba, at a speed frightening to many, soon proved to be fundamental.[7]

Each step of what is called the Cuban Revolution has been an immediate response to a need. The peasants need their land: *give it to them.* The children need schools: *build them,* and improvise "crash" courses to make teachers—many of them hardly out of childhood. Rich property owners in the cities charge rents that make them millionaires: *put a ceiling on rents* and turn the balance over for construction of new non-luxury apartments. The oil refineries could stifle the economy of the island and immobilize the rebel army by cutting off the oil (as they did in Guatemala): *take over the oil.* The United States government punitively balks on the sugar quota: *sell the sugar where it can be sold.* Russia is friendly (for whatever reason): *be friends with Russia*—leaving the door open, however, for friendship with the United States.

No imported dogma, no alien doctrine, inspires Cuba's transformation. But this does not mean that Castro's men have been unaware of economic theory. They have studied it, learned

7. A recent version of the change to prevent basic change is the President's offer of great sums, beginning with a half-billion dollars, for "The Inter-American Fund for Social Progress." The money will help the poor of America Hispana; it will not change their basic values. It will certainly not prevent the shift of power and control in the hemisphere away from the United States, which—as the other Americas know—is the true motive of the grant.

from it. The innocence of the Cubans, performing impossible feats of reconstruction at impossible speed, is nothing but the magic of a *changed attitude*. Cuba is rich in all men need for a good life? Cuba belongs by right to the Cubans? Very well: *give Cuba to the Cubans*.

The magic is that it appears to be working! Cuba could be murdered; one hydrogen bomb might do it. Castro could be murdered; he is a conspicuous and open target, with none of the protective trappings of a dictator. (His freedom of movement is as remarkable as was that of Lazaro Cardenas, Mexico's great President, who nationalized the oil and placed the Mexican peon on his *ejido*.) There is confusion and disorder, of course; the Cubans are human. Often, what is majority social justice works injustice for individuals and groups, who become enemies—perhaps sincerely convinced enemies—of the regime. (This is the inevitable by-product of social revolution.) The reforms themselves are bound to create internal difficulties in the future, with which the elections of tomorrow will have to grapple. People will be hurt (some for good reasons, some for bad), will disapprove or will hate. And, of course, the cold war of the United States will strain ever more deeply, as it stimulates ever more fiercely, the resistant powers of the new republic. As we shall see, there are also favorable items for Cuba's situation in a world so largely beseiged by similar demotic forces.

For the moment look beyond Castro and his problems, at the youth of Cuba. It is easy to see them, everywhere, in Cuba; for they are "running the works." "Where are the old people?" I ask. A militia girl of sixteen replies, "Oh, they are resting." Not merely dearth began this revolution, as Castro's words to the Assembly often seem to imply. Plenty also began it. Not only hard facts of economics began it, but also innocence arrogant and vital—the innocence of youth that can be wonderfully right and perilously wrong—and a great Dream of America, of both Americas, which we must understand if we would know what is happening in Cuba.

1. *History of an Island Full of the Sea*

CUBA is an archipelago, and archipelago means a sea studded with islands. The stress of the word is not on land, but water. Cuba, like Greece in the Aegean, has thousands of isles called keys, hundreds of harbors that lead the sea inland. Cuba has also mountains, but the long land is so narrow that mountains are lookouts upon sea. Water is Cuba's constant presence.

Lying on the edge of the Tropic of Cancer, Cuba is cooled in winter by the fresh trade winds from the north. It is a link between the torrid and the temperate zones, a liaison land on the routes from the North Atlantic to Mexico and South America. So Spain regarded it and used it. So the eighteenth- and nineteenth-century statesmen of the United States almost without exception, from Benjamin Franklin and Thomas Jefferson onward, viewed it: a bastion of defense for the liberal Anglo-Saxon culture and finally (they were all certain) a goal of American conquest southward.

The people of Cuba were formed by this aqueous land. They lived near water and it suffused their nature. They lived as a threshold for kingdoms far more important to Spain (Mexico, Peru) suffering and profiting from neglect by the mother country.

The sea is man's past. Life sprang from it. Yet a man's face immersed for more than a minute brings death; and a man's body under its vast weight is soon crushed and devoured. The sea is simple, and it would be quiet but for forces—moon, sun, winds—that wrench it into currents and stir it into waves. Man in his present knows his past in the sea; knows that his blood is salt like the sea waters and that his body is a member of the sea. He beholds his past destiny in the sea, and loves it;

beholds in it his threatful present and future, and fears it. He turns his back on it, building his dry home away from the sea and against the sea.

The sea is gentle as he scans it; and it allows his ships safely to negotiate upon its gentle breast. But the sea beheld by the man of Cuba is the mother of the hurricane. The waters are gathered up, spiraling into sky which becomes wind and water, feeding each upon the momentum of the others until the wind-roused waters are a whirling, circling violence ready to crush the earth's surface, and to crash against the mountains until they break as if they were fragile as the antennae of an insect. All this the man of Cuba knows, without words, who looks upon the quiet sea surrounding this island, upon the sea within his island, and upon the hurricane sea within himself.

When Columbus sailed into Cuba, and on later voyages sailed almost around it, but not far enough to know it was an island, he found dwellers whom he learned to classify into three groups, each with its language.[1] The first of these, who came to be known as the earliest dwellers there and the most primitive, were the Guanajatabey, whose chief utensils were shells: conchs of marine univalves and bivalves, for pots and other kitchen use, and also sharp shards of broken conchs for weapons of attack. But this was a minor usage: these were a meek and docile folk. They occupied large parts of Cuba (having come isle by isle from the north coast of South America), but when the Spaniards found them, they were confined to the western end of Cuba.

The Siboney, successors of the Guanajatabey, were differentiated from them chiefly by their wide use of stone artifacts. The group of Siboney preponderant in Columbus' time, the Taino, made pottery, ceramics, skillful stone sculptures

1. In questions of Cuban ethnology, I have relied upon two of Cuba's leading and most trustworthy historians: Ramiro Guerra y Sanchez, who quotes M. R. Harrington's *Cuba Before Columbus,* and Fernando Portuondo del Prado. Despite many differences among them, all the authorities agree on the plurality of Indo-Cuban cultures and languages already noted by Columbus.

and ornaments of gold and copper. Haiti, Jamaica and the Bahamas above them were occupied by the Taino, as was most of Cuba. They were a people of the sea in its gentlest aspect. To the explosive Europeans they seemed idlers. When the Spaniards appeared on their easy island, their first response was neither anger nor fear. They wondered, and they welcomed. They touched the armor and the arquebuses, like curious children, in glee. And when they saw the passion of the Spaniards for gold, they gave what they had gathered in the rivers; when they observed the need of the Spaniards for women, they lent them their women. To attack did not occur to them, until they were attacked; and then the fury of their surprise almost disarmed them. They carved their amulets and idols in the hardest wood or in stone; and although far inferior to the work of their neighbors, the peaceful Maya, their art resembles it. They may have carried on commerce with the great cities of Yucatan and Guatemala, across the narrow strip of sea.

But they spoke in dread of a very different race eastward from Hispaniola, a race called Carib. This people's culture centered upon war—and desire for war. They had slaughtered their way north from the delta of the Orinoco, and from such islands as Trinidad, through the Lesser Antilles, and already had secured a foothold on the east coast of what is now Puerto Rico. Even today, there are Carib villages in northern Venezuela, near the peninsula of Paria, which it is unsafe for a white man to visit. They have never acknowledged the republic or learned Spanish. "Carib" is their own word for *brave,* and the favorite game of the young bravos is to shoot uninvited guests. The Caribs had no civil laws, for their constant state was war. They hunted beast and man. They were the hurricane, and it has meaning that the Spaniards named the southern half of the American central sea "the Caribbean." Spain, whose theory was to bless all Indians as potential brothers in Christ, excepted the Caribs. They were judged carnivorous beasts, to be shot on sight.

All the races that inhabited Cuba suffered decimation at the hands of the Spaniards. Bartolome de Las Casas, the good padre who became the Indians' official defender, may have exaggerated in estimating at 300,000 the number of natives in Cuba when it was settled by Diego Velazquez, first captain-general of the Caribbean (1512). But at the end of the century, there were only 4,000 survivors! What had destroyed the others? An occasional massacre when fear brought panic to the Spaniards. Cruel slave labor. The Spaniards' possession of many women, whose offspring were *mestizo* (mixed). Most of all, the spirit of servitude which the Indians could not suffer. They vanished, therefore, and bequeathed the same passionate need for freedom to their mestizo children. A fiercer hurricane than the Caribs had swept the island.

When they were almost gone, the Taino rose in revolt. They were led by Hatuey, a Taino chief from Haiti. They had on their side the jungle heights of eastern Cuba; but they were naked, and their arrows could not penetrate the Spanish armor. Their hands were feeble against firearms, swords, heads encased in helmets and the terrifying charge of horses. Most crucial: the diffused social will of their race could not meet the sharp ego of the West, secure in its immortality and its conviction that all nature and all earth was its God-given right. Hatuey was captured, tortured and invited to become a Christian. He declared that he did not like their *cacique*, Christ, judging him by the conduct of his men. He preferred to burn at the stake, loyal to his own lord. This was the end of the Tainos. (Today, Hatuey is a hero in Cuba, and a popular brand of cigarettes bears his name.)

The shape of Cuba, which is 750 miles long and 50 miles at its widest, has suggested the alligator to the Cubans. Its head is the eastern province of Oriente, massive and tilted down from the body as if the beast were about to plunge below Haiti and Puerto Rico, to rip their soft bellies with its mountain teeth. Its snout is at Baracoa, its visible eye with the head seen in profile is the Bay of Nipe, and one forward leg is the peninsula of Cabo

Cruz. Its body, with the back grazing the Tropic of Cancer, is the land from Camaguey to beyond Havana, and the long tapering tail of the beast is the western province of Pinar del Rio. Close to the tail are Florida to the northeast and Yucatan to the southwest; and the brute seems to be trying to escape them.

The alligator is a savage beast. It will lie motionless in shallow water, nostrils dilated, eyes hardly visible, and when the prey—mistaking it for a log—comes close, the jaws snap shut. It usually drags its mass through the mud, but challenge can move it to surprising and lethal speed. It is indolent, immobile, hardly visible—and bursts into sudden carnage. The alligator is an element of the marginal sea, and lives within the minds of the men who live within that sea. The benign Taino, the ferocious Carib, the lusting will of the Spaniard, the torpor of estivation and the hurricane's insane bite—all are traits of the history of Cuba.

Cuba is also called the "Pearl of the Antilles." According to the *Encyclopaedia Britannica,* "the experience of pearl-fishers shows that those shells which are irregular in shape and stunted in growth, or which bear excrescences, or are honey-combed by boring parasites, are the most likely to yield pearls." "Pearl" is a metaphor with meaning, since Cuba, surrounded by the mother Caribbean, has been irritated by the Caribbean's centuries of invasion, piracy and exploitation.

But there is another figure of speech for Cuba which suggests a deeper meaning. Reverse the alligator whose head is the province of Oriente; look at Cuba now as pointing northwest into the Gulf of Mexico, where the two Americas meet, and Cuba has the shape of a phallus. Its scrotum is Oriente (the former alligator's head). In erection it points northward and westward, penetrating the widely open vulva of Florida and Yucatan toward the immense womb of the Gulf, whose north shore represents Anglo-Saxondom, with Mexico—Amerindia— closing in upon the west and south. These are the mother organs. Cuba's thrust into them then symbolizes the new impetus of revolution from the east—Cuba, Africa, Europe—upon the mother Americas, both old, both superseded, which nevertheless must shape, as the mother shapes, the unborn, the newcomer. The old "New World," Hispanic America as it has been and the United States as it has become, both obsolete or obsolescent, are threatened by the seminal act of Cuba, as the mother's world is always threatened by the new world of her child.

Fertility is a parabola. No one knows what the birth of Cuba will be, or what it will lead to, except that it will be American. Therefore the old Americas—equally to the south and to the north—resist it. In the terms of our metaphor of the phallus, Florida and Yucatan, representing the two Americas, are vulva leading to the womb of America's future, and they have been fertilized by Cuba.

The old dreams of brotherhood, justice and plenty, shared by the whole hemisphere, have found new tools and new techniques that will determine the new civilization; for aim and means always determine goal. This is the vital task of our time: to judge our aim and means. Man has intuitive knowledge that it is the nature of the means by which he moves toward ends which makes his life, and that *ends* are never reached, because *means* change them and dissolve them.

Cuba has become an aim of humanity incarnate—as Russia is an aim, and Israel and China and the new Africa; and as the United States was a world aim in its great days of Washington and Jefferson. One cannot control the course of the parabola of birth. No one can know what the *new* will be in Cuba. But we can obtain hints by knowing in depth the present character of Cuba—can know something of the new child, knowing its parents.

The first fact to note is that Cuba from the beginning was not typical. No two of the American Captaincies and Kingdoms of Spain were identical. Mexico was not like Peru, although at conquest both had Indian cultures of high quality, which by their contrasts differentiated the resulting Hispano-

Americans, who were neither Amerindian nor Spaniard. Chile, with its never-conquered Araucanians and its Andes conquered only by the air, was not like Argentina, whose immense rivers (watery pampas), set it off from Uruguay—which in turn differed from Paraguay, whose Guarani population has given it a nature remote from its neighbors'.

Nevertheless there was, with all its variations, a general pattern to the vast realms of Spain. They were, most of them, as Spain judged, immense successes; and Cuba was a failure. The conquerors sought gold and silver. In their sacramental religion one substance became another, and by an easy analogy the Spaniards mistook gold for wealth and power. Christianity, by permitting ego to invade the meaning of the immortal soul purified and saved by Christ, released the huge energies of egoistic mercantile and national capitalism. And Christianity in Spain, with its sacramental psychology, exalted gold as the magical conveyor of earthly riches. But gold was scarce in Cuba.

The first Cuban colony, founded by Columbus, was massacred and burnt by the natives. Doubtless the excesses of the Spaniards in their futile search for gold played a part in the outrage of the natives. When a little later Hernan Cortez led his small company from Cuba to Mexico, and, finding gold, broke the Aztecs, the Spanish settlements in Cuba were almost deserted. Mexico became the goal, and then Peru. Cuba, poor in the glory of gold and silver, was reduced to humbler livelihoods: diversified farming, the raising of tobacco and some sugar, above all the raising of cattle.

By the beginning of the seventeenth century, Cuba's central plains, where the grass stood man-high, had become cattle ranges. The land, technically the king's (*tierra realenga*), was loosely apportioned into estates, whose earnings were too small to justify the surveying of boundaries or the fencing of the lands. Small farmers squatted and settled within the estates' borders. When their children grew, the small farm multiplied. These estates were not organized enough, not strong enough, to have lobbies in Madrid. They were not in the class of the huge *latifundios* from Mexico to Peru. Within the century the economy of Cuba differed from the typical gold economy of the rich Spanish-American kingdoms, by the profusion of small independent farmers and by the *laissez faire* relations between them and the larger, yet still comparatively modest, *hacendado*.

Spain was so little concerned with the potentials of this new Cuban order that it restricted the production of tobacco because it did not want to be troubled selling it in Europe. The first revolts against Spain in Cuba were not, as elsewhere, slave rebellions (Indian or Negro), but the uprisings of literate, individualistic tobacco growers, who acknowledged the king but condemned his government. This was a pattern to be frequently repeated.

Soon the Cubans were answering Madrid's legal restriction of trade to commerce with specified ports in Spain by dealing illicitly with England, France, Holland, and above all the thirteen booming British colonies of North America. Smuggling became larger in volume than the fixed quotas of trade with Spain. The "free" trade soon got mixed with the rivalries of navies, for war was almost continuous between Spain and the other countries. The distinction between legal raids on enemy lands and the huge activities of pirates became blurred. In 1600 there were thousands of buccaneers working in the Caribbean. They raided the gold-galleons from Mexico and Peru. But they also concluded pacts with the governments in Europe, which often made the leaders naval officers, even giving them titles, such as Sir Francis Drake and Sir Henry Morgan, titles which would be given also to the successful businessmen of a later epoch.

Cuba's function in the big boom became that of a transition port, a sea-policing station. Havana, Santiago and lesser towns on Cuba's munificent coasts became full-fledged commercial cities along the long water roads to and from Mexico, Panama and the Continent southward, or along the east coast to Argentina and through the Strait of Magellan to Chile. By 1600 there were eighty taverns in Havana, and a whore for every sailor. Pleasure is as essential to commerce as defense is essential to it.

Almost at once the Caribbean colonies of France, Britain and Holland had become factories of sugar, for which vast numbers of African slaves were brought in. The slave business, which often yielded 100 per cent profit on the investment for a single raid, was largely British. Attempts were made to convert Cuba into a sugar factory. Britain tried it when in 1782 it won Havana from Spain, holding it for eleven months. The attempt failed, and did not succeed until the Americans took over, in 1898. A typical British sugar island was 90 per cent Negro. Cuba's black population never exceeded a quarter of the total population, except for a brief time when it was a third—considerably less than in several Southern states.

British Barbados in 1925 had 180,000 Negroes and 14,000 whites. French Haiti, before the slaves rose and massacred their masters, was over 95 per cent Negro. British Jamaica, with 870,000 blacks, was ruled by 7,000 whites. Similar disproportions are found in all the exclusive sugar islands. The Negroes' cultural handicap *in no way* implies a basic superiority of the white race. A land with 800,000 whites ruled by 10,000 Negroes would have the same cultural disadvantage. The predominant race of a nation must determine its culture. Where a small minority rules and the majority are held to inferior status, cultural impotence and malnutrition follow. Cuba was saved from this imbalance.

Long before the United States shackled Cuba within the iron frame of sugar monoculture, a frame smashed by the Cuban Revolution, it had become culturally conditioned by an open economy of free farmers, large and small, and of towns that dispensed services to its own people and freely (although illegally) did business with customers abroad, notably with England and with the Thirteen Colonies soon to be the American republic. Sugar was there, but not exclusively. And of course, the term "free" is relative. But in economics and political mood, Cuba differed deeply from the greater colonies of Spain; and in its preponderantly European ethos, differed from the slave-run factories of the Caribbean. To its mistress, Spain, it was not a success. And this failure, during the formative sixteenth and seventeenth centuries, is one of the causes of its becoming in our time a people and a nation.

To find another theme of the land we must turn again to Spain: not this time to the Spain whose ego reached rampantly for limitless horizontal goals, the Spain of the ego which is dominant in modern Europe, but an earlier Spain of a Semitic quality which the Christian gospel awakened throughout a Crusade, eight centuries long, of Christian northern Spain to drive out the Moslem. This strain is not primarily of Europe, but of Africa and Asia Minor. It is the note of *prophecy*. Spain has it through its two great Semitic populations: Arab and Jew, both peoples of a prophetic culture. And Spain has it through the Bible, through the Jewish, Christian and Moslem schoolmen, and through the great literary mystics rising as flame in "the Dark night" of St. John of the Cross.

We shall hear this Semitic theme of prophecy not only in Cuba's prophetic poets. Jose Maria Heredia and Jose Marti, and in recent singers, Nicolas Guillen and Alcides Iznaga; not only in the generals of the Thirty Years War with Spain, Maximo Gomez and Antonio Maceo; but also in statesmen and warriors of the present revolution.

Don Quixote, commanding figure of Spain's literature, is, of course, the Semitic prophet at odds with the modern European civilization that was replacing God with Ego. He strives with his whole life to translate his mystical knowledge into conduct and action: into an *ethic,* as Spinoza (of the same family) defined it. This is the effort of Don Quixote, fighting for social justice and for love. And it is a myth so hopeless in terms of the modern world that Don Quixote—lean, impoverished knight of La Mancha—becomes ridiculous: a joke, a failure. But the myth is so nourishing, so embracing and exalting, that a hemisphere draws life from it. More than once, perceiving Cuba, we shall think of Don Quixote.

Before the sixteenth century was over, contemporary Cuba was already present in most of its basic substances, dynamic and potential. There was the sea of the slow tides and the hissing hurricane, there were the soft nurturing trade winds and the alligator. The Tainos were gone, but their swift vanishing itself was still present: the guilt of it, the pity of it, and the relief of it, too, for the Spaniards did not want them. When the island was first settled, Santiago and Baracoa were the principal towns, useful to ships coming out of the East and touching Cuba at the east. But before that century closed, Havana had become the island's principal city, equally useful, since the services of ships passing to and from the West had become the primary function of the island.

The pirates were already virulent; the French Huguenot Jacques de Sores (like Drake, more buccaneer than officer) plundered and burned Havana in 1555, and by the turn of the century the freebooters, enemies of Spain, were setting up little "states" in Caribbean islands. They represented more than they knew: the anarchy of a dissolving medieval order; the wild release of energy and will within egos convinced they were blessed souls to whom all nature had been given, all power sanctified by God—with no method, no psychological techniques to guide them. In the north (France, Britain, Holland) this was true also, and from the seventeenth century onward in the Thirteen Colonies of Britain. The forms differed, not the elements. In the north, the liberated ego was free to turn to science, to mechanical invention, to the huge enterprises of commercial magnates. In Spain's empire the energy was caught by the Counter Reformation and the imperialism which called itself "of Christ," which aimed to absorb the earth. Unleashed ego was in the Jesuit communities of South America no less than in the little Zions of New England; in the Spanish lust for gold no less than in the expanding paper monies of the bankers; in the rituals of the exclusive churches no less than in the wealth-producing machineries of the new industrial nations.

A diversified economy of cattle and mines, sugar, tobacco, coffee, gave the Cubans not freedom but some air within the Spanish frame. The surrounding islands were already factories of sugar: factories whose cylinders and pistons, lathes and wheels, were human—the dark flesh of the slaves whose blood provided lubrication. Everywhere, the factory, the machine, and the pirate will of magnates were spreading.

No one, of course, in those early centuries of Cuba, dreamed of the United States and of the immense, concentrated power it would bear upon Cuba. The United States was not yet present; but all its psychological and cultural premises were present.

2. Saint with a Sword: Jose Marti

IN 1853, in Havana, Jose Marti was born, a man almost as comprehensively representative of America Hispana as a single person would be comprehensively representative of Anglo-Saxon America, who had made the contributions respectively of Jefferson, Lincoln and Walt Whitman. Cuba was progressing. Already in 1837 there was a railroad from Havana to Guimes, a rich sugar district thirty miles southeast. Another line was built in 1842 to Matanzas on the north coast east of Havana, and before the close of the 1850s tracks linked the capital to Batabano (south), Guanajuay (west), Cienfuegos (southeast) and Camaguey at the island's center. Landowners prospered, and sugar was not Cuba's single money crop. Smuggling with the United States was a larger business than the sole legal trade with Spain, whose shifting governments, despite the theory of Cuba as a province of the metropolis, handled it more and more as a military conquest. Many of the landed gentry favored Cuba's annexation to the United States, whereby they would have profited from the aggressive politics of the slave South. But in 1868, when Cuba's Ten Years War began, slavery in the United States was gone; and the manifesto of Cuba's first republic—the *"Grito de Yara"*—backed by two hundred landowners in arms and headed by Carlos Manuel de Cespedes, called for the gradual emancipation of slaves with full indemnification of the owners, and for the protection of the island's quasi-feudal freedom.

Moderation in every form characterized these decades. But Jose Marti, who was brought up in them, was conspicuous for his total want of moderation: in his ideas, in his intricate language, in his emotions and his public conduct. The ten years following 1868 was a period of war among semifeudal lords, made ineffectual by the balances between their regions and their regionalisms. The renewed war of 1895 opened and was waged upon a platform of ideals so fantastically high that it sounds more like an epistle of a modern Paul than like the working orders of a revolution. The difference in depth and in heat is expressed by Marti.

Marti's father, a humble Spanish soldier from Valencia, who for a while rose to the post of policeman in Havana, was the acme of moderation: loyal, gentle, generous. Marti's mother, Leonor Perez, native of Tenerife in the Canaries, was the archetypical mother of Spain: deeply forming, demanding nothing. The bright boy went to the municipal public school, and absorbed before his teens the seditious doctrines of his teacher, Rafael Maria Mendives, who played a role in the education of Marti somewhat like that of Simon Rodriguez in the education of Bolivar. Mendives was exiled to Spain. The boy, at sixteen, was in the Presidio, in chains, and working under the blazing sun of the prison quarries. The labor was too much for the slight body and brought hernias, from which he suffered all his life, and ulcers where the iron manacles gored into his legs. In 1871, when he was eighteen, he too was sent to Madrid.

Spain's methods in punishment are revealing. If a Cuban criminal was bad enough, he was shot or garroted. If he deserved to live, he was sent to the mother country. To exclude him, alive, from life in the Hispanic world was deemed an unnatural torture to which not the worst must be subjected.

In Spain, not yet twenty, Marti wrote a play, *Abdala*, whose theme is love of country, and a book on the terrors of his life in the Presidio of Havana. (A fragment of the Presidio walls still stands as a memorial to the sufferings of Marti. Nearby is Morro Castle, and beyond is the Cabana, a prison for criminal enemies of Castro's republic as the Presidio was for enemies of Spain's kingdom.) Marti's book was not suppressed—nor did Spain reform the Cuban prison. This, too, is typical of Spain:

this blending of ferocity and freedom, of realism and disdain for realism's conclusions.

In Madrid and Zaragoza (Saragossa), Marti studied law and became a lawyer. The Cuban war collapsed, chiefly because of the dissension of the local leaders, who refused to take orders from caudillos of other cities or to lead their troops beyond the borders of their particular province. Marti was free to return to Cuba. That he had not tried to escape from Spain to join the war; that instead he had remained in Madrid, writing articles and a book on Spain's dread Presidio, troubled Marti until his death, as his death will reveal. But he had witnessed Spain's own attempt to achieve a republic, and learned how little it improved Spain's pathological attitude towards its one great remaining colony. From then on, Marti's passion and devotion for Cuba's independence did not waver.

The frustrated war had produced three exemplary military leaders, who became part of Cuba, part of the inner life of Jose Marti, although as yet he did not know them. Calixto Garcia, well over six feet tall, was herculean of body, beautiful of face. His father had been a wealthy Venezuelan rancher, who had settled in Cuba's Oriente Province, in the city of Holguin, where the son was born in 1839. He was too restless to go to college. He loved good food, and women. His wife, in matriarchal fashion, raised their seven children and several others illegitimately sired by Garcia. Cuba's independence became the principle of his life and when the struggle broke into the open, he rose from the ranks swiftly: a virtuoso of a fighter and a chieftain of fighters. Hearty as a Rabelais, devout to his cause as a saint, he swept the rich eastern land. He disliked the orders of his commander, Gomez, to destroy the property of Spaniards, for he loved all blooming and all life; but he obeyed his superior.

In 1875 the war began to collapse, and Garcia was threatened with capture by the Spaniards. The prospect of a long prison term was unbearable to his dynamic and potent body. He aimed his revolver upward into his jaw, and fired. By a miracle, he did not die. The bullet touched neither his vocal chords nor his brain, but came out at the forehead, leaving a deep indented scar. He spent four years in prison. But when the unsuccessful war was replaced by the uneasy Pact of Zanjon, he refused the false peace and organized a continued resistance, which came to be known as "the Little War," *la Guerra Chiquita.*

It was a failure. The Cubans were not ready, and their chief soldier, Maximo Gomez, warned against premature renewals. These were unhappy days for Garcia, days of forced patience. When at last he met Marti, in New York in 1882, he was discouraged.

"I am tired," he said, "of fighting for a cause in which my compatriots do not believe." Marti heartened him, explaining this "unbelief" as the weariness of confusion. Garcia the superb, with the mark of a miracle upon his forehead, looked at this civilian in a black suit worn threadbare yet without spot or dust, and saw the head crowned by dark chestnut curly hair, the great black eyes and the domed forehead. Within the mean and humiliating poverty of New York, Marti seemed to be living an imagined Cuba of free men. Garcia should have looked down on Marti, who had not fought the war, as the man of words looked up to the soldier. But Garcia felt a luminous authority: a secret numen. Cuba's poor human forces were dispersed among the oppressed at home or abroad, exiled from New York southward to Mexico and the Caribbean. Feeling Marti, Garcia knew these forces were not poor; this man held them together and transformed them; and wherever he went, Garcia took Marti's affirmation with him.

During the Ten Years War, a Negro, humble-born in Santiago (1845), rose from the ranks swiftly under the discerning eye of Maximo Gomez. Antonio Maceo became a brilliant cavalry officer, fighting an intricate war against the largest European army ever to cross the Atlantic. As he fought, he planned the tactics and strategy of offense through rivers, jungles, mountains. Gomez made him chief of operations, in full command in Oriente. He was a tough, lightning-swift fighter; but his letters to his wife (he had no formal education) reveal that from the start he had a prophet's sense of Cuba's democratic mission and his own privileged destiny within it. Maceo never stressed and never forgot his origins. The war in Cuba was to him the struggle of all men to be free, and the Negroes were men. He rode relaxed into battle, and came from the field equally relaxed and alert. He did not drink, did not smoke, and permitted no profanity in his presence. His beard and moustache were always carefully trimmed, his dress was faultless. Fate had made him the herald of his race; he performed and looked his part, which would not end until a final bullet reached him.

Marti's third commanding possession was Maximo Gomez. Gomez was not a Cuban. He was born in the Dominican village of Bani, of pure Spanish, comfortably situated parentage. The date, supposed to be 1836, is uncertain, for the baptism papers are lost, and some of his biographers believe it should be set back four or five years. The new state of Santo Domingo was the scene of constant civil strife, with periodic invasions by Haiti. The young Gomez was among those who invited Spain back to reoccupy the country. In fact, the young man's first visit to Cuba was as a sergeant of the Spanish army in Bayamo. He saw with anger how the Spaniards maltreated their slaves, resigned from the army, and became a revolutionist. The transformation was briefly before the war of 1868, and Gomez at once offered his experience to the insurgents. While he was explaining to Cespedes and his staff that good will was not enough to make good soldiers, the news came of a column of Spanish cavalry approaching the camp. He asked for permission to deal with it, maneuvered his raw troops, and wiped out the column. His rise was swift. His impulse, it appeared, was a passionate hatred of oppression and a virtuoso's joy in battle. He was keen, swift, primed with tumultuous energy, fearless and devotedly a democrat. Also, not less important, he was lucky. Five horses were shot under him; twice he was wounded.

(Maceo's body was entered by twenty-two bullets before the final one, which killed him.) Undoubtedly, the fact that he was not Cuban-born saved Gomez from some of the wrangles and jealousies of regional caudillos. He could be irascible without losing his poise; indeed, his sudden squalls of temper, bringing sharp and pithy words, were tactical parts of his war methods. He kept his tattered army under constant observation, and his soldiers, feeling his warmth and his intelligence, accepted his scoldings, for they knew he loved them. When the first Ten Years War failed, the captain-general of Spain in Cuba, whose aim was reconciliation, offered Gomez a large sum to establish himself in business. He refused, and worked for a time in Jamaica as a common peon. But he discouraged both Maceo and Marti, who were in a hurry to begin again. When Garcia launched his "little war," he condemned and would not join it.

Gomez looked more like a schoolmaster than a soldier. He wore steel-rimmed spectacles, even in battle, a gray goatee drooped over by a full moustache, and a constant kerchief around his neck in lieu of collar. He looked old when he was young, and never aged. In the war of 1895, when he was at least sixty, he was still deft and swift in the saddle. Experts agree that he was a brilliant strategist. By speedy tactical movements, he multiplied the striking force of his troops, who never exceeded 30,000, most of them poorly armed, against the final 240,000 troops and the comparatively limitless potential of Spain.

Gomez knew the position of every Cuban and every Spanish soldier. Without roads, through the abbreviated jungles of thorny brush, impassable without the machete, he kept in touch with his own men and with the enemy. But Gomez was far more than a fighter. His wisdom, his tenderness that came from it, his detachment for ruthless action, and his political clairvoyance (he saw the trouble for Cuba brooding from the American North) were human traits of excellence. He was not an easy man. Twice during the war, and once just after it, the Assembly removed him from office. He accepted the demotion, and offered his services in any subaltern post. But his leadership was needed, and he was soon reinstated.

Marti wrote him for the first time from New York in 1882, urging preparations for war. Gomez replied bluntly from Honduras, where he was training the army: "The time is not ripe." Two years later, they met in New York and quarreled. Gomez insisted on the need of absolute authority and command in revolutionary war. Marti rebelled against what seemed to him capitulation to the theory of dictatorship. The means, he said, must not be alien to the end; if it is, the means wins. Gomez cited the fatal regionalism of the leaders in the first decade of war and Cuba's impotence to finish its long, tragic business of revolution, if the present anarchy of authority continued. Arrogance was in his voice and his words, which seemed to put the young civilian in his place. Wounded, seeking to hide his hurt, Marti strode from the room. What followed marked the mettle of both men: Gomez, left alone, reviewed the arguments of Marti and found them correct; recognized his own arrogance and made ready to confess it. Marti, alone with his sorrow and his pride, realized that his pride had spoken—and his envy of the soldier. Each wrote a letter of reconciliation to the other. From that day on Gomez was with Marti, and Marti was in possession of the heart and mind of Gomez.

3. *Freedom Is a Poem: Marti's Death*

IN January 1880, Marti came to New York, his home (with many visits to other American cities) for the fifteen years before his death. He had been exiled a second time to Madrid, escaped, had seen Paris in winter, tasted London, and had gone to Mexico—which he gave up, after considerable success as a writer, because of his hostility for Porfirio Diaz, President-dictator. In Guatemala, likewise, he got into trouble with the reigning general. In Venezuela, he became *persona non grata,* after he had refused to praise President Blanco Guzman in a public memorial volume, by which the dictator sought to prove that the intellectuals were with him. Marti knew the islands of the Caribbean. He knew America Hispana. Wherever he was, he made his way, teaching and writing articles for such excellent papers as *La Nación* of Buenos Aires. Now he was to know the United States, and to interpret it with a depth of understanding never before within the reach of Hispano-American readers. He earned his bread by working in an export house, Lyons and Company, and he had a single-room office at 120 Front Street for his revolutionary affairs. In Mexico he had married Carmen Zayas, a daughter of a rich bourgeois family in Camaguey. The union was not a success. His wife was disappointed in her "visionary" husband, who could not "let things be" and who failed to provide for her as she expected. With their boy, she frequently returned to Cuba; always coming back to her husband, always leaving him again to his solitude and his revolution.

Marti wrote: "May the limits of love not cast a spell on the earnest ambitions of my mind." He wrote also:

Con los pobres de la tierra,
Quiero yo mi suerte echar.
(With the poor of the earth,
I choose to cast my lot.)

He was in solitude, not because he lacked companions of both sexes, but because he was preoccupied and busy. He experienced the deep loneliness within plurality: the fate of men who know their unity with others. In an article on Goya, he called *La Maja Desnuda* "voluptuousness without eroticism." This characterized himself. His overwhelming passion and devotion was for the cause of Cuba. He held meetings as far afield as Tampa, raising money and kindling enthusiasm in his Cuban hearers. From time to time, Marti wrote a poem. But these were not "occasional" poems, not "patriotic" pieces. Cuba was never named in them. They were the essence of his consciousness as a man. The poems deepened, becoming at last masterly works, whose resonance at times recalls the limpid yet complex music of the great Spanish mystics, and presages the sculptured sensitivities of Ruben Dario.

His speeches, delivered before humble workers, mostly *torcidores* of tobacco, revealed a baroque splendor of image, a wealth of associative thought, that transformed the cause of Cuba into a universal value. The journalists of Spain sneered at this exalted prose of Marti. It was not Spanish, they said. Marti became known, jeeringly, as "Doctor Torrent," or "Señor Cuba Weeps." One critic wrote:

If the body (of the piece) lacks thought and coherence, its form can hardly be considered a product of the Castilian language; it is rather an *uprising* against the Spanish syntax.

Indeed, his prose is not easy. It is an architecture of many substances, with the single gravitational force, which in buildings holds the materials together, replaced by a variety of pulls and stresses in all directions. A prose page of Marti is often, in the dynamics of its parts, as intricate as a chess game in full play. Not Spain, and not America, had known such prose. (Possibly the spoken versions were simpler than the published. Even Cicero is supposed to have rewritten his orations before letting the world read them.)

In conversation Marti's voice was low, subtly warming. In his speeches, the voice swelled with the context until at the climax it was oceanic. In the published version this voluminous surcharge is produced—in lieu of voice and mobile body—by the syntax, which Marti's critics quite rightly called "not Castilian." A statement opens: at once tributary statements are ingrafted, and contrapuntal ones, shaping, reshaping, transfiguring the original indicative substance. And at the close of the long sentence, something of cosmos has been infused into the bare statement, making it an experience: organic, human.

Marti's poems, meanwhile, matured toward simplicity. There is no eroticism; the voluptuousness is refined into what a man might feel before the slender body of a scarcely nubile girl, whom he dares touch hardly with his eyes.

Meanwhile, this man lived humbly in Brooklyn, crossing by ferry each day to his dusty, cluttered office in New York, where the names of Cubans and organizations of Cubans who wanted Cuba to be free were filed away. Close by was the seaport with its spicy airs—Whitman's Manahatta—and Wall Street with its bankers and brokers, for whom Marti was not even a name, although he knew and feared them. Close, too, was the whole continent in the mind of this man, who already in 1880 loved Whitman and Emerson and Thoreau; knew the strengths of Cleveland and Tilden; divulging it all to his readers in Caracas and Buenos Aires. In 1877, with false papers made out to "J. Perez" (his mother's name), he had spent a secret month in Cuba—his last visit until the final one. Since boyhood and the Presidio, he had lived mostly out of Cuba. Now he traveled to the American towns where Cubans worked: raising hopes, raising money, organizing links between *émigrés* and key men in Cuba. He kept his own expenses down and saved. On boats he went third class; in towns he stayed with friends. His letters to his wife reveal his thrift—unto parsimony. In his eloquence, his deep knowledge of what was good in the United States— and what was evil ("I have lived in the Monster, and I know it," he was to say in a letter)—and in his countless articles and interpretations of every country on the American continents, he was sumptuous and lavish.

When Marti first lived in New York and Brooklyn, he was far less known to the scattered Cubans than the older men, the soldiers of the Ten Years War, headed by Gomez, Antonio Maceo and his brothers, Garcia, others. By 1890, Marti was in correspondence with local leaders in every Cuban town, and all the Cuban communities in the United States knew his soft voice that could rise to hurricane force, the touch of his warm hand, the knowledge and love in his large eyes. By 1891, when the *Partido Revolucionario Cubano* was formed and prepared for war, Marti was the inevitable leader, with none more devoted to this choice than the veterans. Now also, the poems finally deepened. In the same year that made Marti Cuba's revolutionary leader, his *Versos Sencillos* appeared, followed the next year by the *Versos Libres,* a prosodic integration of what he called "the huge incoherence of America." In his foreword, Marti wrote: "I love the difficult sonorities, the sculptured verse, vibrant as porcelain, fleet as a bird, ardent and overwhelming as a tongue of lava."

This comment, harbinger of the modernists to come, ignores the chief trait of the mature poems of Marti: their *springlike* energy and fragrance.

The accent is on spring, on the energy of spring. No doubt one could find in the annals of the West politicians who were masters of good prose; poets and prosemen who were deedfully concerned with politics. Lincoln, Bolivar, Caesar, wrote great prose and were men of action. Dante was involved in world politics and wrote great poems. But such exemplary men, whose plays were cast on grandiose stages, do not match the subtle quality of the achievement of Marti. He was a poor man, a man with no "connections." His black coat and his linen were frayed but always clean. He suffered until his death from the hernias and ulcers dating from his prison years.

Alone, half-deserted by his wife, painfully longing for the presence of his son, who was growing up without him, from his humble and insecure position in a powerful country that opposed all he loved but did not know he existed, he mobilized a people disheartened by defeat and by its isolation among the sister-republics that were too weak and too afraid to help it. This people, dispersed and alone, he organized and launched into knowledge that it was a nation. And meanwhile, in prose of remarkable complexity and music, he conveyed his experience of the modern world to these nations who were not yet of it, and wrote poems that make him a prophet in literature as he was an apostle in politics.

Marti studied finances and the problems of illicit arming. (It was, of course, illegal to ship arms to be used against Spain from the United States to Cuba.) He slowly collected a treasury: the humblest *torcidor* of cigars gave his dollars, and the small manufacturer of cigars his fortune (in one case, $50,000). As the eighties vanished into the nineties, a problem was to guard against uncoordinated actions; here Gomez helped more than the impatient heroes, Maceo and Garcia. And Marti's greatest problem of all was to sustain a detachment which could preserve his strength and guide him. Like most Hispanic revolutionists, Marti was anticlerical. (The church was never strong in Cuba, and Marti had joined a Masonic lodge while in Madrid.) Here his cosmic sense, the natural mysticism of his origin— Semitic Spain—sustained him. He kept the whole scene intact before him: Cuba in *his* America, his America in relation with the North and the whole Western world. Marti knew Bolivar's sense of American destiny, not because he had learned it but because it was in him.

Soon, with terrible urgency, he would need it. But the light that truly led him was his love for the bodies of life: a flower, a child, a docile peasant, the island of growing glory. Through his sensing the beauty of these, he touched God. And as the enemy of God, he feared the untidy violence of Cuba's history, fatally induced by Spain, inevitable with Spain's presence, and now lurking under the mask of North American "progress."

By the end of 1894, Marti was ready. The pennies and the dollars of the devoted had bought materiel and ammunition. In the little port of Fernandina, Florida, three small vessels stood secretly loading. One would go to Santo Domingo to call for Maximo Gomez and his two hundred picked men and carry them to a small port in Camaguey Province at the center of the island. One would go to Costa Rica for Maceo, Flor Crombet and other valued veterans of the earlier war and convey them to Oriente, easternmost province. The third little ship would sail direct to the province of Las Villas. The Cubans at home had been chosen and instructed. They knew what was coming and what to do: each in touch with his own district, none in knowledge of the details of the entire operation, except Marti. The loading of materiel was finished, the ships were ready.

By stupidity or treachery, one of the men boasted about the plan to a seller of ammunition. Frightened, he told the police and the police told Washington. The three ships were embargoed, and Marti was arrested in New York.

To Marti, this was disaster. Would it be disaster to Cuba? The ammunition was lost, and the guns, and the three vessels. But the towns and countryside of Cuba had been alerted; it was too late to countermand orders which required several days to execute and which already were moving. A halt now, in Cuba, would mean demoralization. With the courage of the man who sees the whole, Marti fought his rage and his anguish. Although the ships were held, there was no direct evidence against Marti, and he was released. He went on with the plan, however maimed, which was to get to Cuba and to send other men to Cuba. He needed Gomez, and he intended to see him at once. But he needed, no less, a platform for the revolution. When he reached the Dominican village where Gomez waited, he had the first draft in his pocket of what became known as the Manifesto of Monte Cristi.

Gomez in his diary notes the cool and contained temper of this man who had just suffered in Fernandina what seemed the collapse of his work of many years. Gomez writes:

> After informing me in all its details of the loss of the three vessels, we began to study what we must do to resolve so difficult a situation, in view of the few resources we could count on.

The document the two men completed that March of 1895[1] in the plain village house, in the bare room with a pine desk, painted red, to work on, was a strange declaration of war. It reads today more like an academic paper on social responsibility. It insists on the need of war to oust Spain from Cuba, and on no less a need that the war be conducted without hate—and speedily, with destruction and death minimized. *"Una guerra culta."* It studies the unfortunate republics of America Hispana and ascribes their frequent failures to the fallacy of their trying to adjust themselves to "alien models"—meaning the United States. It studies the race relations of Cuba, the collaboration of equal men, and decides there can be in Cuba no "race problem because there are no races." "Cubans," it says, "are ready to be free and to rule themselves." It studies the cultural aptitudes of the Cubans and finds them exalted. It calls on the Spaniards in Cuba to become Cuban citizens, or to remain neutral in a conflict they cannot contain, or to die without hate if they cannot leave Spain's army. The fighting ahead becomes almost incidental. Let us get to work, the manifesto says, to forge *viable forms* for the republic. It envisages Cuba as the node of a network of free nations, rich in the commerce of the world, free to advance toward brotherhood of man. A romantic paper! Its insistence that the Spaniards can never hate the Cubans

1. It is interesting to compare the manifesto with Bolivar's great Angostura address (1819).

since the Cubans cannot hate the Spaniards is a romantic threshold to violence; and reads more like the peaceful fantasy of a dreamer than a call for war. Yet these two men had lived in violence, military or civil, and were quite ready to meet it again and to die for their dream. This paradox is part of the energy and quality of Cuba.

On March 25, they signed the manifesto and prepared at once, somehow, to get to Cuba. Cuba was waiting. The loss of ships and ammunition did not change this. The synchronized invasion by the veteran leaders and their picked men had been frustrated, and it was a pity, but to Marti, Gomez and the others the *body* of the revolution lived in Cuba, waiting, strong as ever. The signal had gone wrong, no more. They needed merely to readjust the signal.

Gomez and Marti, with four others, got to Cuba together: a secret and difficult undertaking. They had to buy a boat, a large dory, and to bribe the skipper of a tramp steamer to drop them, their equipment and their boat into a heavy sea. In the launching, the tiller broke and they had to steer by oar. At last, in the dark night of 3 A.M. their dory scraped bottom: land of Cuba!

"Joy was our feeling," said Marti's letter to a friend. And to his wife: "*Solo la luz es comparable a mi felicidad,*" "Only light is comparable with my happiness." They were at a beach called Playitas, on the extreme southeast tip of Oriente, due south of Baracoa. They saw lights beyond the thicket. Enemy lights? Friends? Heavy laden they pushed toward a *bohío,* a typical hut-home of the poor Cuban peasant. This was their best chance. They burrowed in the brush and waited. Dawn came swiftly. The *bohío* door opened. An old man came out, saw them, knew them and cried "Brothers!"

They were nearly a hundred miles east of Santiago. All Cuba lay before them. They had aimed well, hitting at once on a brother, because, they were sure, all Cuba was alive with their brothers. Maceo, they soon learned, was already in Cuba, and Bartolome Maso, and many other veterans.

On May 5, they met at a sugar mill called *La Mejorana*. Marti stressed the need of an immediate civil government with representatives elected by the people. Maceo, skeptical of civilians in a war, wanted—until the fighting was over—a junta of generals with one civilian secretary. Two thousand troops passed in review, and Marti addressed them. He had been at most a name for them. When he concluded, they stood—as an observer put it—like the children of Israel listening to Moses. Gomez was chosen commander-in-chief; Maceo was his lieutenant in command of Oriente, the most revolutionary province. Marti, delegate of the Revolutionary party and chosen President pro tem of the nascent republic, beamed with joy when Gomez gave him the honorary title of major-general.

The plan of Gomez was to leave Maceo in charge of Oriente and proceed at once to Camaguey, the island's center, in order to release the revolution there. Marti went with him. The generals, subtly embarrassed, told Marti that his duty was to return to New York where he alone could master the problems of coordination, finance, supplies and foreign relations. Without his continuing in New York, the revolution would remain a maze of fragments, never reaching the strategic, concentrated strength to end the war. Gomez knew the difficulties. Spain had well-equipped professional soldiers, and the ports and ships to bring in more. Gomez also knew the threat of intervention by the United States if the war dragged on. All this Marti knew, of course, and even better. Could he fail to know that in New York he was indispensable, but not in the field? Marti stayed on.

May 19, on their way westward, Gomez and his small escort reached Dos Rios, at the confluence of two rivers, the Cauto and the Contramaestre, northwest of Santiago. Marti was writing letters to his mother and to friends. A little before noon, a scout rushed into camp to report a Spanish cavalry column racing toward them. Gomez ordered Marti to stay in camp and ran out with Maso to command his men. But Marti, left alone, found his horse and followed. The charges of the two columns balanced on the field, and both withdrew. Gomez returned to the camp. On the field, Marti lay dead.

The men people call great are symbols; a people speaks through them, although their immediate motives appear individual and circumstantial. This is the mysterious way of our organic world, whose members are not conscious of the links between them. Cervantes may have believed he was satirizing novels of chivalry and the archaic *pundonor* of Spaniards losing a world they did not know. Yet through his book, the modern age revealed its alienation from its Judaeo-Christian past; revealed that to love God and to do justice in its present meant to be as ridiculous as Don Quixote. Marti's self-exposure to battle, for which he was not trained, and self-withdrawal from the work at which he was adept, may be drawn in psychological terms. Having staged a war in which blood must flow, should he not incur the risks to which he exposed others? He had long suspected (as was voiced by his political foes) that only a veteran of the Ten Years War had the right to bring war back. Perhaps Marti was wearied of his role of agitator; perhaps he longed for the relative simplicities of the soldier. And perhaps he wanted to die, knowing that if he lived he must face, for Cuba, problems more frightening than Spain. His last letters appear, in retrospect, to reveal a presentiment of death: they were farewells and literary testaments. But this proves nothing: any conscious man goes into battle knowing he may die.

Nevertheless, Marti's death—as perfectly as his life—becomes a symbol. Marti is Cuba. Cuba is this at last articulate island in which the deep, the high, the obsolescent culture that was Spain has agonized; has been neglected, exploited, and violated until it must die or be reborn—in a new body. This culture-spirit was too vital to die. And it was not ready to live. The sweep of Marti's pen reveals its limitless potential. The casual skirmish in an obscure corner of Cuba where Marti came to his end reveals cruelly its fragile fantasy. Cuba was not ready to be what Marti meant by Cuba. Cuba was not ready for Marti —or to be Cuba.

They buried him with tears, the tough veterans, the fresh recruits, who had just come to know him. His *guerra culta,* the "detached war" in which Spaniard and Cuban were conscientiously to kill within a cosmic knowledge worthy of the Bhagavad-Gita, remained on the printed page of the Manifesto of Monte Cristi.

The *insurrectos* totaled at most 30,000 men, with machetes and obsolescent rifles, until they began to take from prisoners or the dead Spain's excellent Mausers (manufactured, ironically, in Argentina). There were railroads only from Havana to Las Villas and Cienfuegos. Roads were poor, with nothing in the whole land to match Cuba's stately highways of today, arbored by *ficus,* lined with royal palm and laurel. The prowess of Gomez, Garcia, the Maceo brothers and such leaders as Maso, Moncada, Ruloff and Grombet, was in the cavalry charge: the frenetic riders with machetes lacerated the infantry of Spain and vanished into jungle brush and sierra, where their foe could not follow. At the juncture of the provinces of Havana and Pinar del Rio, and between Camaguey and Oriente, the royalists dug a line of trenches with periodic forts, called *trochas.* The trenches were flooded, and rigged with barbed wire; the forts, of wood, had room for a score of sentinels, and these *trochas* spanned north-south from sea to sea. Their aim was to bottle up the raiding rebels, but it did not work. In consequence the Spaniards were always on the defensive, always on the run; Gomez never gave battle except on his own terms. The Spaniards were strangers to the land. And (not least) they were subject to malaria and the still mysterious yellow fever, which, it is estimated, killed over thirty thousand Spanish soldiers.

The fighting became savage. Gomez ruthlessly ordered the burning of every barn and field owned by Spanish sympathizers. The Spaniards did as much to the rebels. The peasants served the rebels, giving them food and information. The Spaniards held the cities; but intellectuals, professionals, and more than a few among the humble priests favored the republicans. The method of the Cubans was similar to the Blitzkrieg of the Germans in 1939, with horses in lieu of tanks, making demoralizing raids into the depth of enemy territory, isolating and infuriating the towns. The temper in Madrid grew short and ugly.

Spain's captain-general in Havana, Arsenio Martinez Campos, was a *caballero* accustomed to the rules of civilized war—with the same disgust for the cavalry raids of the rebels as that of orthodox French generals for Hitler's tanks and planes. He saw no issue to a war lacking the structure of battle, except through slaughter of noncombatants. For this, he had no stomach. He resigned, recommending to succeed him General Valeriano Weyler, nicknamed "the Butcher:" true forebear of the Nazi strategists. In 1896, Weyler came to Havana with reinforcements and a plan. It was the peasants who kept the rebels going, with food, with supplies, with spying. He rounded them up and herded them behind barbed wire in concentration camps on the outskirts of large cities. He burned their farms, wantonly slaughtered their cattle, and made no provision for feeding them. (Here too, note the analogy between Weyler and the Nazis.) Over a hundred thousand men, women and principally children died of starvation—on a rich, vast island with only a million and a half inhabitants. Unfortunately for the dutiful and competent soldier of Spain, the Spaniards at home did not like his methods. He was praised as a loyal servant—and recalled to Madrid. But the damage was done, Spain's American rivals for Cuba had their pretext.

Before Weyler's recall, photographs of *reconcentrados* had begun to appear in the press of the United States. The American people, sitting down to breakfast in their comfortable homes (big, American breakfasts) saw staring them in the face children who were skeletons with distended bellies, naked old men with rigid eyes, mothers in rags with empty breasts for their nurslings. Motives of conquest and empire doubtless possessed the politicians, such as Theodore Roosevelt; the newspaper proprietors, such as William Randolph Hearst. Without *their* motives, doubtless, the American people would never have seen the photographs or thought at all of Cubans. Nevertheless, the American people were decently horrified, humanly angered. All they needed was to be able to forget those pictures while they enjoyed their breakfasts.

4. The Face of Revolutionary Cuba

THE sea comes so strongly into the city of Havana that the stones and stucco appear liquid. The water penetrates to the inner harbor, with the Castillo del Morro a passive sentinel to the invasion; but the mists, the heat and the cool trade winds from the northeast, are modulations of the sea. The old cathedral and its neighbors near the water present a massive mood of defiance; they stand against sea as eternity against time.

The sea fluidity is in the people. Havana "flows" easily; is always on the brink of demonstration of its watery substance. The people gather readily together, now that the country is theirs, *campesinos* (peasants) among them. The crowd listens to a speech, but its fixity is an illusion; a right word—or wrong—will release it. Havana has an instability like waves. But like the ocean waves, instability is not the depth of the matter. Winds may ruffle the sea, sun and moon make shifts in it; but deeply within itself the sea prevails. And despite its flimsy new structures, its cluttered invasion by American goods and gadgets, Havana prevails: a city sufficient to itself, partaking of the permanent sea although violence, as of the rushing waters of the hurricane, may shake it.

The old houses of the narrow streets, the new ones along bright avenues, are washed by the sea air and painted by the sun: white, cream, saffron, pastel blue. But a grime has come upon them. Havana is like a white yacht which the crew has taken over: a crew more interested in the problems of navigation through dangerous waters than in elegance. Even in its buildings of earlier times Havana shows its change of purpose.

In architecture Havana has never been distinguished. The cathedral is clumsy baroque without the authentic splendors of

the baroque in Mexico, Ecuador, Peru. The Morro fortress is
the conventional rampart which Spain set up as the British
menace to its islands grew; with none of the power and beauty,
for example, of the great fort at Cartagena. The old streets
avoiding the sun, full of moisture and darkness, have savor
rather than distinction. And the new streets rising in the Vedado
are at their best when trees hide them. Here are innumerable
establishments for tourists, garish with neon lights that blink a
broken English. Here are the new hotels of the Batista era,
lavish with ultramodern decorations, for the most part in good
taste. All this—the villas too—is international Havana: not because it is only for foreigners, but because the Cubans who
owned most of the houses and gave the nightclubs most of their
business, in one way or another played the game of the foreigners in Cuba. They shared in the wealth of sugar, they helped
reap the largely foreign harvest of the utility monopolies; as
bureaucrats, politicians, vice-impresarios and business men they
gave to Big Business the collaboration it relied on and was
ready to pay for, in order to drain billions out of the country.

The corruption of *Cubans* in Havana reveals much. On the
surface it is conventional. In the old port basin, as in every
water front, there are the sink cafes of whores, pimps and
thieves, where a few treats of rum will pay for dances torn from
Cuba's centuries: Africa and the slave ships, the wild assault
of pirates, the still more cruel indifference of rulers. These cafes
have no stage; the dancers act out their passion on the floor,
whirling, kneeling, lying in barely disguised postures with an
abandon less controlled and closer to the onlooker than the
candomble dancers in the back hills of Brazil's Bahia. If, however, the tourist wants to be safe (for in these sink cafes the
line is thin between play and deadly violence), he can go to
resorts like La Tropicana where the same meat has been steri-
lized and canned. Anything to please. The responsiveness of
Havana is like the responsiveness of water yielding to gravity,
to wind, to temperature, to color . . . and infection.

During the eleven months of the British occupation (1762)

more than ten thousand slaves were introduced into Havana, tilting the town toward the sugar monoculture. Havana never returned to its old loose order; but it never went forward to the goal of Barbados or Jamaica. It responded and remained itself. In the nineteenth century, Cuba turned toward revolution. *Spain must get out:* this was the island mood for a whole hundred years, and rebel movements rose in all the provinces—*except Havana.*

The struggle was fierce. The Cubans burned the cane fields and the sugar *centrales* (mills) and the tobacco crops of the Spanish sympathizers. Spain's army, which grew to over 200,-000—the largest European force ever to invade America—was desperately on the defensive. Finally Spain herded the Cuban peasants, who had been feeding the rebel army, into the camps of the *reconcentrados,* where the old men, the mothers and the children, starved and diseased, died by the hundred thousand. Havana remained beyond this struggle.

Peoples, like individuals, have their pathology. Havana's "absence" for a hundred years from Cuba's history can be explained only on the premise of a populace alienated from its country and its true nature. When the young organism is biologically ready for maturity, it must mature. Delay is danger; delay prolonged is disaster. During the entire nineteenth century, Cuba needed to mature as an independent nation. External wills, principally the insistence of the United States that Cuba remain Spain's until it was "ripe" (in the words of John Quincy Adams) to "fall" into American hands, thwarted its normal organic growth. In Cuba this meant anguish and tragedy; in Havana, the most conscious part of Cuba, it meant alienation, which produced political and cultural corruption. The alienation went on, after the founding of the false republic (1902). It meant the absence from government of the men of integrity who could not accept the lie of independence. It meant the presence in government of those who accepted and exploited the lie. Even architecturally, the alienation was visible—for, as Lewis Mumford has said, "Architecture cannot lie." Witness: the monstrous capitol building, utterly unrelated to the life of Cuba, aping the alien capitol in Washington; the dapper and pretty villas of the rich along Havana's Quinta Avenida; the business skyscrapers, Egyptian, Moorish or both together; the Bacardi building, which in its lobby of dark marble and bright bronze irrelevantly resembles a mausoleum of baroque Rome.

Where was the true Havana? If not in the dapper streets, perhaps in the old ones soft as rotting mangoes; or in the old plazas where the unemployed lounged and drank their poverty-cocktails, sugar and water and alcohol. The metropolis of a land may be its antistrophe, as Paris to France. Or like London, it may dream under its soot of again being part of vernal England. Or like New York it may be a prophetic symbol of the fate of the whole land. Havana articulates the peoples' past alienation. Close to the Morro and the ancient prison in which Spain and the dictators after Spain kept their enemies, and where recently the worst criminals of Batista's army met their fate, rise the two great oil-refinery chimneys. They send broad swaths of sticky smoke into the air, faintly blurring the lights, soiling the stone and stucco. The winds spread this soot over most of the city. It is a small matter, and a symbol. The refineries were built with alien money, and they were placed where they are, for easy and cheap access to the port. Havana's luminous light and the glow of its citizens, as they enjoyed their island's loveliness each morning, were not considered.

The mobility of the Habaneros has always been gay and easy. They got along even with the British. The bitterest foe of Washington's Department of State will smile (and sincerely!) when he meets a *Yanqui* on the street. Only the seven baneful years of Batista wiped the smile from Havana's face and kept it from its play and its night clubs. Havana is in its streets again. But still not active, as the provincial Cubans are active for their revolution. This is because Havana feels too much, not too little. The provincials who sustained the armies during the nineteenth-century wars of independence knew in simple terms what they wanted. During the revolting years of the false republic, they knew they were not getting what they needed, what they wanted. They are simply sure they are getting it today. Havana never knew what it wanted. And knows too well what it does not know, to be secure and without anguish today. For it knows that *now or never* is the hour of Cuba's birth. Cuba must live as a mature republic *now;* in deep intercourse with a mature America Hispana and with a world of mature republics. It knows that maturity delayed brings anguish; hence the seemingly hysterical hurry of Castro and his colleagues, which is practical wisdom.

The new gaiety of Havana has a depth it never had before. Tragedy is in it. The Cuban church has never been strong, as it is strong in certain other Hispanic countries. But the Judaeo-Christian sense that life is tragic and that the good is to be attained only *beyond* tragedy, pervades the people, whatever the Cuban individual's attitude toward the church dogma. Watch the marching boys and girls of Cuba's new militia, which is to replace a national army; hear the Havana pavements ring with the firm footsteps: you will feel the dimension of the tragic in the present gaiety of Havana.

On September 28, 1960, Fidel Castro returned to Havana from the Assembly of the United Nations, where he spoke for four and one-half hours. Placards had been put up on Havana's central streets inviting the citizens to welcome their leader at 6 P.M. before the National Palace. But great crowds, including thousands of *milicia* youths and girls, in buses, trucks and on foot, had gone the twenty miles to the airport at Rancho Boyeros in order to welcome him sooner. When the plane landed, there was silence, suddenly bursting into song: improvised song of pleasure. Castro was rushed by his staff into a closed car where the people could not touch . . . could scarcely see him. He objected and changed to an open jeep. Now, with the reverent reserve of a church procession the people stood, letting the jeep inch forward. The road to the city was thickly margined by the people. They waited patiently; when the leader appeared they cried, "Fidel! Fidel!" and when he was out of sight the youth marched homeward, singing half-humorous songs:

> *Fidel, Fidel, que tiene Fidel,*
> *Que los Americanos no pueden con él?*

(Fidel, Fidel, what is there about Fidel
That the Americans can't handle him?)

> *Fidel seguro*
> *A los Yanquis dáles duro.*

(Fidel, sure thing.
Makes it tough for the Yankees.)

Long before Castro appeared at the National Palace, three hours late, the Prado and the streets approaching the little plaza were flowing with men and women: not close-packed except on the converging avenues, for Fidel's voice, loud-speakered, would carry far. When he appeared, with President Dorticos beside him, the thousands who could see him gave a great satisfied roar which ran, a huge wave, to those who could only hear. The first voice, the President's, was received with attention: Dorticos is a great orator, a learned lawyer and highly respected. But the applause was subtly removed from the expectancy which was for Castro. One felt a reserve, as when a woman in love for some good cause kisses a friend or near relation *before* she greets her lover.

The black-bearded hero in gray-green uniform took the place of the groomed and shaven President, and as his voice lifted on electronic wings, a process began organically distinct from the mere delivery of speeches. What Castro was saying was sometimes true—all too sadly—as when he spoke of the shameful reception his delegation received from New York hotels;

sometimes it was uncomfortably demagogic, as when he declared of "American imperialists" that "not a thousand of them are worth one honest Cuban."

This was an act of two equal organisms: one a man receiving value from symbiosis with a mass, one a mass receiving from symbiosis with a man—an act of blood and body whose union became spirit. Fidel would round out a paragraph; the people would roar receiving it. Then they would sing. Then Fidel would continue, again silenced when the crowd took over. One could almost see, as one could feel, the embrace between them: the give and take of physical adjustment so wide it moved all Havana. The crowd purred, roared, sang in joy of union; the speaker roared, purred, and the beat of his measured phrases upon the body made a song.

There is a link so strong between this man and this folk that it holds even when Castro speaks on television; even when he addresses the cool U.N. Assembly, a thousand miles away. This is the kind of jointure that makes heroes: men who totally voice their people. It is an event that has its peril. The intimate, immediate embrace could become necessary to Fidel; *make him an addict.* And there always come times when the embrace is wrong; when the leader must dare for the people's sake to oppose the people. The hero's vision must transcend, not only embrace, in order to meet a need in depth which the people cannot see. A birth is always as fragile as it is great. "No man," said Bolivar, Castro's predecessor, "is great with impunity." The relation between Castro, his people and his word is vulnerable, because it is greatly human.

But we return to Havana: there were obvious causes of the capital's backwardness in rebellion. Spain had its main forces there: soldiers, functionaries, Spanish money. Misery, therefore, was more remote. Under the corrupted republic, the privileged economic and political classes made Havana their stronghold. But although this "explains" the inactivity of the Habaneros, and such failures as the general strike called by Castro in the mountains, it does not remove the deep cause: alienation and self-suppression. Now, whenever Fidel spoke, Havana responded. And Havana was not now Spain; not now the false republic tolerated and controlled by Washington. Havana also was now Cuba.

Castro's speeches, beginning with the famous one of 1953, *History Will Absolve Me*, cut below the separateness of Havana and Cuba, making them one. The peasant in the Sierra Maestra, 700 miles away, lived for the first time—through Castro's movement—with the city clerk, walked with him, and they were ready to fight together! The army of Batista was a carefully trained body of men (trained and equipped by the United States), whose existence depended on the suppression of the people. Sadists, who exist in every land, were inherently drawn to this army. But these Bastista soldiers were Cubans. The words of Fidel and his actions louder than words began to decompose this army. The dissolving process reduced the efficiency of the state's military forces; the residue was broken in battle and in guerilla warfare. There have been few successful revolutions, like this one, in which the rebels prevailed over a loyal national army.

If you follow Havana's Fifth Avenue westward; follow the procession of houses of the rich: the dapper, the motley-colored, the banal and the *outré*, you come to Marianao. Here are splendid beaches and a Coney Island park. Here Batista spent over 800,000 pesos[1] of the people's money to build an exclusive yacht club—a snug basin against the blows from the Gulf—and a club casino smart as the best. Of course, the people never saw this establishment or its beaches. To get in, you paid an initial thousand pesos. But to be a member you had to be the kind of citizen who approved of the kind of government which spent almost a cool million for a club and a beach that barred the people.

The club, once the Biltmore, is now a Circulo Social Obrero and its name is *Cubanacán*, the Taino word for "heart of the island." For an American it is a remarkable sight, for it is full

1. One Cuban peso equals one U.S. dollar.

of Cubans of all colors and kinds: workers, of course, but there's no bar against shop-keepers, professors or even poets. Indeed, my host is Nicolas Guillen, greatest of Afro-Cuban poets, who has built from the matrix of his forebears' fierce rhythms a passionate, contemporary living substance.

It's strange to see men who are obviously humble workers playing golf on an elegant course which was built for tycoons or perhaps a U.S. President. Elsewhere a large group of men are learning Judo from a huge barefoot Japanese who commanded a squad of suicide planes in the last world war. Girls, young mothers, fathers and children are spread on the once exclusive sands and in the water. On the floor of the main building's basement lie hundreds of paper bags, the sort you get at the supermarket, containing the clothes and valuables of the bathers. I was told no theft had ever been reported; nevertheless, a year from now this room will be full of lockers.

The bar and dining room are crowded. At the tables, on the porches or on the beach, there are plenty of celebrants of the Sunday, long before lunch time. Beer is a common beverage, but although I stayed until late afternoon, I saw no individual with a trace of alcoholic behavior. Perhaps the drinkers were defended by another intoxication.

There must have been many more than a thousand men, women and children making holiday, seething with a half-uttered music. As the day rolled on under the sun, the inward music grew more explicit. Most of these people were young, and their predominant note was jollity. Everywhere, little clusters broke into song, a spontaneous combustion. Guitars appeared; bongos; a trumpet or two. Boys and girls together began subtle steps of dance, the foot hesitant forward, the head marking a caesura. This is a typical Cuban pattern: a step that is veiled in hesitance and suddenly breaks out, yet with the violence contained. There is a famous night-club singer in Havana, Lupe la Loca (Mad Lupe), who flings herself into an orgasm of motions. She bespeaks a decadent Cuba whose explosive senses express frustration. This scene of Cuban workers and their children is more typical, and their gaiety has restraint, an ever-present sentiment that life is tragic.

By mid-afternoon, the crowd—those not in the water—are gathered up into the processional music of the conga, which has spread like a cool cane fire. The words aren't much:

> *Esto solo se da en Cuba,*
> *Nuestro club Cubanacán.*
> *Cubanacán can can*
> *Cubanacán.*

or even more brief:

> *Viva Cuba,*
> *Viva Fidel*
> *Y todos los*
> *Que lucharon con él.*

A little orchestra comes together, like metal chips in the field of a magnet. A "maestro" comes forward, spontaneously, to head the conga column. Boy and girl stand in tandem, their entire bodies subtly aquiver, until they receive the command to move slowly forward. Where I stand, I can see the variety of faces: the stern and strong Hispanic, the African of sinuous power, and blendings hieratic as ancient Egypt must have had. The wonder is, they belong—without emphasis—together. Each dances in an absolutely perfect rhythm—a rhythm not of dead conformity but of variation—with the sense of parabolic energy beyond, still virgin. They are not dancing to reveal their social unity; the unity is the base, the premise, of their dancing.

All levels of assent coincided in this miraculous rebirth of Batista's yacht club. "We are Cubans, and Cuba is ours," their improvised conga said. But *they* forgot it. "We are human beings," was the implicit meaning of their holiday.

The air here was clean. Havana was too far away to send the smut of its refinery chimneys. Up from the beach with the salt and the spray rose a human vibrancy; its penetration intense but not assertive. The vibrancy of Cuba can be unbearably keen; can even be unbalancing, provoking neurosis or psychosis. Not here. The transformation of the club from a deed of human exploitation and of man's cruelty to man into a simple and spontaneous haven of men and women sharing the mystery of life seems to be perfect. How long? Until what and when? I cannot say. But here is a true moment.

Beyond Marianao, with its miles of dwellings various as a show of abstract paintings, is Mariel, where live a couple of young Cubans, handsome fellows with firm, beautifully formed lips, slender bodies and keen eyes. They used to run a night club on the outskirts of their little town and harbor. Do not be surprised at a night club in so unlikely a place. The Cubans love dance and music even more than they love baseball. The neighbors, however, humble workers living in long rows of one-story wooden houses, without glass in the windows, found that the club kept them awake at nights. They protested and the club was closed. What should the boys do? They had a mother and her mother to take care of. As club managers, they knew the plethora of empty and useless bottles. In their home they fixed up a lathe, a grindstone and a little faucet of running water. They cut off the necks of bottles, rounded and smoothed the lower parts into glasses and tumblers of interesting shapes. These they sell for two pesos the dozen.

There are typical elements of Cuba in these two young men: their ingenious use of waste materials, their invention of a simple machine to help them in their essentially *handmade* venture, their background of song and dance, and under it all themselves . . . intelligent, resourceful, gay yet severe, caring for *madre* and *abuela* and making just enough money to take their girls to a dance at the nearest night club with no neighbors who object to the noise.

Cienfuegos—Trinidad

Cienfuegos is a modern city, founded in 1817 by men who wished to profit by its harbor, one of the broadest and best on the south coast of Cuba. Before dawn, in the empty streets with a breeze from the surrounding waters, one feels . . . one almost sees . . . the spirit of the city. The buildings express it. They are mostly of two stories, pale without the pastel colors of more stylish towns in Cuba. The outskirts have tints and hues; for example, the recently completed Hotel Jagua (it was begun in the days of Batista), with its huge lavish halls, its gray-painted corridors and balconies, which bathe each bedroom in sea-borne airs. But the center streets are dull, monotonous white. An hour after the sun rises, seeming to take heat from the earth, this whiteness is invaded by the people. The proportion of Negroes is the usual quarter-to-third (in Oriente it is higher); but the effect of all the people is of darkness. The Hispanic eye is black, the Hispanic hair is black with glinting highlights. The effect of the young women tightly wrapped in bright clinging cotton, clicking along on the silly stilt-like shoes, is of dark flesh. But the darkness is Spain's. I saw a dwarf, not raimented like the dwarfs of Velazquez, but revealing the same life; and I saw a man in rags whose aspiring head suggested a portrait by El Greco.

As everywhere in Cuba, *where are the old?* Youth seems to have swept them out and away, or boarded them up in shuttered rooms. But the electric quality of the young people transfuses the city with hot darkness. In temperature, in resilience, in color, the population of Cienfuegos—as the population of Havana—are distinct from the buildings. They do not *live* in their banal nineteenth-century houses; they pass in and out; they stop, of course, to sleep, to shop, to make love. But they *live* in a different matrix.

The matrix gives them both security and air. They are a happy people. For centuries they have suffered: true, but their gamut of pain was strictly within their matrix, which could become dark carapace. This matrix is a tradition: therefore it is fixed and rigid. But in their freedom of moving around in it, they have been daring, experimental.

This matrix-carapace is their church and their culture. For four hundred years it has shielded them. They often denied the church; in no country of America Hispana were revolutions so closely allied to the Masons as in Cuba's nineteenth-century wars. Today as yesterday, the church has little power, compared with its immense hold on Mexico, Brazil, Peru. Nevertheless, the church is part of the matrix within which the Cubans have *plenty of room*. They have no direct influence over this rigid dwelling of theirs,[2] but it has vast influence over them. It shapes —or misshapes—them. It is, to change our metaphor, the huge momentum of a colony that was for four centuries neglected, invaded, exploited, at last embraced with desperation as Spain's greater colonies fought free, and finally forced into the deformity of monoculture and unemployment suitable to American investment.

Now the matrix and its carapace are broken. The people with their elasticity, their gaiety, break through. Is this a contradiction? Were the people gay when Machado or Batista cut them down? Did the citizens of Guantanamo have a good time, contemplating the U.S. naval base? The cutters of the cane which flowed billions of dollars into the pockets of absentee owners: were they—out of work for nine months of each year— bright laughers, when they lacked a square foot of soil of their own to plant for their hunger? The answer to such questions must be subtle and obscure like the aged tobacco leaf of Vuelta Abajo. The revolution of birth now proceeding at full speed in Cuba is, of course, a breaking of the form of the Hispanic culture—or rather, a break-through. But without the earlier cultural nutrition of the church, this revolutionary outburst—so distinct from events in Jamaica, Martinique—could not have

2. Even today, the majority of Cuba's priests are Spaniards. According to recent reports the revolution is trying to reduce their number.

been. Cuba's past, beneath and beyond the violence, was a womb of growth.

The shadows of late afternoon cool the central streets of Cienfuegos. From the shops come the women, each one compressed into skirt or slacks and bra, which give her buttocks, breasts and belly a spell sharper than nakedness. A group of *milicianos* of both sexes stand at a crossing of streets under a banner whose huge letters declare: "We approve the Verdicts of the Military Courts." (There has been another of the nuisance invasions of the coast of Oriente: two hundred antirevolutionaries have been caught and a dozen leaders, including three Yankees, have been condemned and shot.) The shoppers mingle with the *milicianos*. A union leader shouts a speech and they shout back: *"Paradón!"* "To the wall of the firing squad." All over Cuba occur such spontaneous meetings as this one. *Reuniones relámpagos,* they are called: lightning meetings. The demonstrators demand death for their enemies, and are having a good time. These animal spirits of youth are ferocious—and frightening. The boys and girls are Christians, but reveal no compassion. They are Christians, but do not accept pity in their need to suppress violently all violent reaction. This is the grim peril under the face of even the worthiest revolution.

To make death present has ever been a factor in Spain's arts. The bullfight, for instance, is founded on the knowledge that here a mortal man *dances,* and by exquisite formal dance makes a beast *dance,* a beast which, if it can, will kill him. Thus the unhappy and misguided men who would destroy Cuba's beneficent revolution must go down to the laughing music of youth.

Follow the Caribbean southeast from Cienfuegos, and soon, as in any part of Cuba, the flat fields rise into sudden mountains. The fields are green with cane and ever increasing rice, are studded with palms—single ones thrusting a fist half-open into the sky—or are paved with congregations of palms, their straight gray bodies and hands outstretched seeming to raise another floor, a green one, above the red loam of Cuba. The Escambray Mountains, rising with their feet in the tide, are massive convolutions of forest and earth together; but their thrust, because they are long and broad rather than steep, is downward. The fields between the shore and the mountains send their powers upward. The cause (and symbol) for this contrapuntal motion is the form of the trees that flourish in these fields. Here is the *agarroba,* with its dazzling spread of branches that rise like intricate fireworks from a trunk leaping up with the countergravitational pose of a dancer whose feet twinkle in the air. Here the prim *bienvestida,* with leaves a-gleam and aglint, whose favorite place is the margin of cane fields. Here the immense *ceiba,* with trunk elephant-gray and pachyderm in texture, broad as a yoke of zebu oxen (its roots a complexity of foot and hoof, half above earth), which on this single mastodon-base sustains a spread of giant branches with small leaves, leaves which darken the earth with their solid shadow for a half-acre. Here the *flamboyant,* with flowers shrill as flutes in January, the coldest month. The total is a counterpoint, up and down, of field and mountain. In a half-coronet of such forces, forty miles from Cienfuegos, lies Trinidad, Cuba's best-preserved colonial city.

Diego Velazquez, first discoverer of all of Cuba, founded Trinidad shortly after 1510, when he reconnoitered the whole island and broke the pathetic last stand of Hatuey. Cuba was now enclosed in the firm matrix of the Hispanic culture. Shattered almost everywhere, it is still intact in Trinidad.

True, it is a bit the worse for wear. The cobbled streets have holes in them. The low eighteenth-century dwellings need fresh paint, fresh stucco, or more. One of the two palaces of the great families—the Brunets and the Iznagas—needs both paint and carpentry repair; the other has been renovated in a yellow finish of bad taste. Soaring above the streets, the clock tower of an ancient convent, a miniature of the Giralda of Seville, has bushes sprouting from its cracks and gaps, and its bell is broken. There has gathered in the inner courts of most of the dwellings the damp of two centuries . . . and the rubbish. Yet the town rises; the final streets become high fields, which become moun-

tains—sustaining on their slopes the *cafetales* (coffee planta-
tions) which gave the town its wealth.

The convent is now a school. The teachers are young men and
women, whose loyalty to the revolution has the pathos of distance, as if the crumbling stones of the old town around them
possessed a more lasting power than the children. How joy-
ously they greet the occasional visitor "from the world!" But
here are older people; and they are on the side of the old walls.
They gather in the cafes in early morning, taking their ease.
(Work is not pressing.) Their archetype is the milkman, who
rides a slender pony on whose flanks the baskets partitioned for
the bottles are fastened; and who cries his milk with a melody.
Perhaps one of the plazas of Trinidad has a loudspeaker to fill
the town with the voice of revolution: I did not hear it. Certainly, there must be many radios hidden away in the patios: I
did not hear them. They are outside the matrix-carapace.

But the violence of the new order is already present in the
lower streets, the younger part of town. These streets are paved,
not with cobblestones but asphalt. Cars and buses rush through
them. There are, however, cheap eating "joints" and lodgings
for those who alight. This is a kind of no man's land, no longer
the old, not yet the young.

One feels in Trinidad the sullen and stubborn presence of
the past; one knows it must be elsewhere . . . everywhere in
Cuba. But one senses no less a symbol in the fresh verdure
breaking and bursting from the cracks in the Giralda tower.

Pinar del Rio and Viñales

The prevailing air of Havana is bland, light and soiled. The
new hotels and office buildings quiver faintly in it, under terra
cotta roofs, as if in an almost bodiless liquor. But the Habanero
is dark, agile, tough. In the old town, one of the noisiest in the
world, the buses, plunging as if to charge the houses, the cars
and the crowds, create a Dantesque pandemonium.

The provincial cities have more unity. Pinar del Rio is the capital of the westernmost province. Columbus called it Vuelta Abajo, meaning "the sun turns down." (The East he called Vuelta Arriba: "the sun turns high.") It grows the most famous tobacco in the world. As you approach the town, you pass the usual motor-age mushrooms: gas stations, garages, eating stands. But the squat central streets absorb the people who move meditatively and thickly like smoke of a good cigar. They are not thinking of Havana, as the Habanero thinks of the world. They are self-contained. The immediate lands surrounding have the color and the aroma of tobacco. Something of the mood of the ancient Indian communing with his twisted leaf, as it goes up from his mouth in smoke, lies in the streets of Pinar del Rio.

Making tobacco in Vuelta Abajo takes about a hundred days. The seeds, selected with exquisite care, are grown in frames, religiously watered, and shielded from the sun. In about forty days they are transplanted to the earth, and a roof—in earlier times of palm leaves, now of cheesecloth—is spread over them. After sixty days of ritual protection, the first leaves are ready to be cut. For the rest of the year the land always lies fallow. Beans, corn, peanuts and other crops would have enriched the loam and fed the workers. The large *vegueros* were not inclined to take the trouble.

All this procedure, based on indifference to the worker, is now on its way out. Cooperatives are already in possession and new, clean dwellings doom the *bohio,* the thatch-roofed shanty, windowless, floorless and dank, which was always the home of Cuba's workers. But the new time has not yet wiped out the old, and the provincial towns are creations of the old. They hold some of the savor of the ritual plant which the Indian cut only at night in the dark of the moon.

There are mysteries in tobacco, the leaf that contains a deadly poison and spells a torpor with hypnogogic images. The tobacco fields, called *vegua,* because they lie low near streams, have their mysteries; and the small towns, where the tobacco workers come looking for jobs when the tobacco work is over, have their mysteries also, as we shall see later.

Not far from the town of Pinar del Rio, there is a valley called Viñales. (Its name is proof that grapes were grown and wine was made in colonial Cuba.) The valley is flat with lush green life, carpeting the red, iron-tinctured earth. And on it stand mountains of strange shape, rivaled only in Malacca. These mountains do not grow or rise from the valley, they are separate upon it! They are vertical; some stand alone, others stand in groups, like a herd of mastodons with huge heads—a quarter-mile above the valley floor. They are of gray calcinous rock, covered by a rugose skin of stunted palms and other vegetation, clinging in the rock's crevasses and cracks. The pachyderm skin covers the whole mountain body, yet its palms and other flora are not found in the valley, and the types of rock and earth of the mammoth bodies are not found even under the mountains. Therefore, they cannot be mere uprisings of the valley. They must have been pushed to where they stand by a telluric cataclysm. And a hundred million years of water's dripping completed the separate cutting of one body from another.

As one looks over these geologic creatures, over their horizontal backs toward the sky, one feels a kinship between them and the vast cumulus clouds. The clouds are perpendicular, as are the mammoth mountains. The clouds in their verticality suggest aspiration, as do the vertical mountains. The human eye, rising with the earth's mountains into ethereal cloud, and with the vertical clouds into the sky's remotest precinct, loses its power of distinction. Earth and cloud are together; earth and cloud become a thrust into parabolic sky, yet are contained within the experience of the mind that beholds them.

In one part of the valley of Viñales, the mastodon mountains herd so close together in a row that they form the side of a subaltern valley. There is a single mountain facade a thousand feet in length and even more in height, paneled by smaller "creatures" at virtual right angles to the main sweep of the bodies. Here, a Cuban artist, Leovigildo Gonzalez, is painting what may be the largest mural in the world. The brush and palms of the pachyderm are already cleared away and much background has been painted in. Already, in fact, a trinity of Indians—father, mother, child—stand firmly forth at the right end of the mural. The left and center parts of the composition will display the organic life which led to the appearance of man. The artist sends up his peasant assistants by immense pulleys, and plastered against the sheer stone wall, they apply the colors according to his directions given from a loudspeaker on the ground.

This gratuitous labor of man, the painting of a vast mural in a remote valley of a relatively remote island republic—a mural to reveal man's part and place in cosmos (its aesthetic revealing also that cosmos is within the man)—tells us much about the present state of Cuba. Even the mountains are being subjected to change; and the change is always for man: from submission to creation. The cooperative farms, the new schools that were once barracks, the new children's cities and low-rent units, the plan of sports for the people and motels for the people are all articulations of a change which, even if it is successful, will bring not the millenium but a mere beginning of man's quest of his own nature.

There were in Cuba, as in so many places of earth, two kinds of peace: a peace of the *possessors* of the land and a peace of *submission* by the others. This peace of submission was frequently broken, but it prevailed among the people; and the possessors, with *their* peace, liked it. Now, both forms of peace are shattered.

Within a generation, they will be shattered throughout the world. This is a transition in the domain of social energy as abrupt as the transition to nuclear physics—and as significant to man. The Sierra de los Organos is a strange body of earth; the cosmic mural to be painted there on a wall of vertical mountains is a strange place for an art form accustomed to the walls of palaces and cathedrals. Strangeness is a door to a revelation. No one knows what the new shape of man will be, if man survives; except that it will surely be strange, if he survives. Even if the Cuban painting be wiped out before it is finished, an incubator and a sanctuary for the strange truth of tomorrow will have been seen in Cuba.

From the anguish of its broken past and that past's peace of possession and peace of submission, a longing lives in this prophetic island.

Matanzas

The Chevrolet sedan rolled swiftly into the first streets of Matanzas. A housewife looked up from the two big paper bags of groceries in her arms, as the car passed her. Her face changed; the ordinary repose of her features was flooded with a light which transfigured the repose but did not disturb it. She said, not loudly: *"Fidel está aquí!"* "Fidel is here!" The two or three men and women nearest heard her, and following her eyes saw whom she saw in the car, now gliding slower than the news from face to face, as men and women saw the man in the car and quickened their steps to follow. Swifter than the car the news now proceeded and spread: "Fidel is here!" Faces brightened, like that of the first woman who had seen him. Nothing rare had happened. Castro is likely to appear at any moment in any place of Cuba. Yet this gathering of light and peace upon the faces was an awakening of wonder, as a dawn of the sun in a clear sky is common and yet a wonder.

The car rolled always slower as the traffic thickened. Castro sat at the right, in front. The driver was a bearded soldier boy, and in back sat two more of the *rebeldes* armed with submachine guns. Behind, but not immediately behind, were a couple of other cars with other *soldados rebeldes*. Now the pedestrians were all moving in our direction. The cars that crossed ours slowed, recognized, and many tried to turn and join the current, causing little knots of interference and wild bursts of klaxons. Side streets condensed as Castro's car drove quietly and slowly. No one shouted, no one had anything to say beyond *"Fidel is here!"*—which meant simply that Fidel must be seen, if possible Fidel must be touched: anyone who sees it naturally profits by a sunrise.

By now not only the streets we traveled and the streets behind us, but the streets ahead were growing solid. The news was a joyous radiation, and our car began to slow because of the thickening before it. Mothers appeared, carrying babes as if to church. And although no one shouted, the mounting of hushed voices, each saying *"Fidel!,"* grew in accumulation to an air pulsant and intense: the breath of the city, breathing its own life, breathed Castro's presence.

Castro continued talking to the man beside him, giving no overt acknowledgment to the people. This was the usual salute he receives, no more exciting after all than the good wife's kiss when her man is home from the day's work. "Fidel is here!" Well, he's always here in one form or another.

The car turns laboriously up a side street and stops before the tall gray building of the local INRA. Once it housed Batista's men, and it still smells of the police. A crowd waits before the door, having guessed Castro's destination. Before the soldiers can clear a way, Castro, agile for a man of so large a body, leaps from the car and plunges into the mass. Hands are thrust forth; he takes them. A woman touches his shoulder. He sees a boy held up before him and shakes his chin. He disappears into the grim building.

It was mid-afternoon. Castro's work meant long and voluble discussions with the local director of the Institute of Agrarian Reform, an untidy, stocky little man with a straggly half-gray beard, who reminded me of Duccio's *St. Peter*,[3] and discussions with this man's assistants. The talk covered an infinity of detailed problems, and flowed on from hour to hour. Castro had much to say, but the others equaled his torrents of words, words that were not rhetorical but represented things: the stubbornness of things and persons in a world-remaking that had no blueprint and that represented people, each stubbornly in-

3. The painting in the National Gallery of Art, Washington, D.C.

dividual, each individually stubborn. The humblest man there had his say, man to man, often with slight courtesy in dissent. I saw no trace of repression, submission or servility.

Lights were turned on, the tall windows shut, and the talk went on. I wondered why the glass windows were so black— were there no lights outside?—and realized of a sudden that they were black with people. They were plastered there, the men and women, shutting out the light, peering in—motionless as shutters. I went to a door; a *rebelde* politely advised me not to try opening it. I heard the murmur, constant and substantial. The people were at every window, at every door: more truly, *Matanzas was there*. It was certainly not hurried; it was simply *there*. It wanted nothing, did nothing, spoke no word. It was a presence, drawn as if by gravity as close as it could get to the lode of attraction within: Fidel, arguing a point with his comrades, as an iron worker, having heated the metal, hammers it to shape.

Suddenly the conference was over. Castro, satisfied, grunted his farewells and strode to the side door. The uniformed boys stationed there opened it enough for us to see the hundred foot passage to the street. It was solid with human bodies. The crowd saw the door open, saw their friend, and their murmur became a vertically-rising shout—*Fidel!*—not strident, not even strong except in mass, and becoming rhythmic with repetition. But no one moved. Castro, whose six feet one makes him taller than most Cubans, looked silently at this sampling of the substance of Matanzas, not disturbed, and *walked into it*. Imperceptibly he moved forward. A hand, an elbow, a torso, a foot, gave way before his impact. At his sides were a couple of the armed boys, but they made no inch for him. They—and we— simply followed his lead, modeling our infinitely slow and steady progress. Carving it. For although Castro was not angry, not disturbed, not nervous, neither was he gentle.

Far beyond us, at the court corridor's debouchment to the street, stood the car, with the crowd almost covering it, and Fidel intended to get there. His body pressed against the pressing bodies. His patient need was to get through; theirs simply to *be* where they were. Therefore his more dynamic need prevailed, with infinite slowness. And no one was worried, except this visitor from the North who—hardly breathing—feared that women and children might be stifled, and who, crushed against chest and loin and shoulder, feared fractures, flesh wounds. There was no ill-humor in the process. There was (with the exception stated) no scintilla of concern. Castro worked his way, and we followed in the wake of his infinitesimal progress. The car came nearer.

Impossible to open its door against the solid mass that did not move; impossible, it seemed, even to breathe. One of the *rebeldes* let himself be hoisted by the mass through an open window. At once he started the motor. I was full of fear. There were women and children, solid like cement hardened. If the wheels turned even an inch would not a foot be crushed, a rib fractured? *"Cuidado!"* I cried out, "Some one will get hurt!" Castro answered me in a low voice, "No one has ever got hurt." The next task was to open the car door. This process was slow as a sculptor's modeling and carving. At last we were all inside, and the car budged. The people must have receded, for we were moving forward at the speed of a glacier, a warm one. The cries at crushed limbs never came. But the crowd seemed as remote as ever from any sense of helping their beloved friend on his way or in his duties.

The relation between Castro and the Cuban people is complex, and complexities alone can help us understand. There is a relation of some sort, of course, between a dictator and his people: a dictation whose will is destruction through brute power. Hate is also in it (including hate of self) although it may be masked as love. Its true nature is revealed by the dictator's fear of immediate contact with the people. Whatever power Castro has at the moment, it is obviously a mockery of words to call him a dictator. Dictators do not act out such intimate embraces as the one in Matanzas. I had witnessed a ritual, not a traffic jam. Rituals have deep roots. And with a phenomenon like this, one is closer to the facts—and their truth—if one gives play to the scene's symbols.

That afternoon I had assumed, as we approached Matanzas, that I would get a picture of the city: the shape and color of its houses, the lay of its streets around its generous harbor, and the lilt of its people at their work and leisure. Of all this I got nothing. A black molten human mass had blocked the city out. Not ill-humored, not destructive, nevertheless the people had blanked the town. More accurately, the docile yet resolute adoration of the people had hidden it. The crowd blocking Castro's way had somehow the shape of Castro. And what was the shape of Castro? Was it not Cuba itself? Was it not *itself*, that the folk loved in Castro? Was it not this presence which *his* presence gave, of a deeper community between each Cuban and his world than the community of a town called Matanzas? The motionless multitude, the motionless leader, and the slow fusing between them barred any vision of the city; for this had been a deeper encounter.

Santiago and the Moncada Barracks

Barracks smell like prisons. Healthy men breathe badly in barracks and the juices of their bodies turn rancid, stale and bitter. Each of the six Cuban provinces under Spain had its *cuartel* and subdivisions: *capitanías, tenencías*. The false republic added instability to the old order of policing the island.

The President, whoever he was, had his hands in the national treasure and the army upheld him—for a price. And the United States upheld the army so long as it maintained the submissive state called "order" and deemed good for business. The system was simple. The public wealth was there to be drained by the politicians, who needed to pay overlords and underlings for protection. Most of the money Cuba made through its great natural resources, Cubans never saw. It left the country and what came back was largely luxury articles for the thieves.

But even the thieves saw little money; they saw only what the United States returned in order to keep a balance of sorts between import and export.[4]

The barracks upheld the President; but if he did not provide for the officers, he was soon in trouble. The soldiers were humble Cubans not satisfied with three months' work each year at subsistence wages on a sugar *latifundio*. They wanted a little more. Fulgencio Batista was a Cuban, humble-born, who wanted a great deal more and got it by giving a little more to the soldiers and the politicians.

There were several ways of reacting to this endemic Cuban situation of rule by corrupt leaders servile to American business and to its State Department. The simple *campesino* did his best to survive, helpless, illiterate, frequently half-starved. The go-getter (typified by Batista and his predecessor, Gerardo Machado) wormed his way into the till by promising favors to the officers, opportunities to the swarming little politicians, and a free hand to the monopolies—mostly American—to bilk the land of its rich earnings. (In a single decade, billions of dollars produced by Cuban soil and Cuban labor left the country forever.)

There were, of course, good and honest men in Cuba, potential public servants. With almost no exceptions, they were left out, or kept out, of office. The lie of Cuban independence, written into the Cuban Constitution as the Platt Amendment,[5] was not digestible to honest men.

The liberals with faith in political reform made a party called Ortodoxo. Its leader was an idealist, Eduardo Chibas, and among his followers was a restless young lawyer, just out of the university, named Fidel Castro. Chibas had a regular radio program. One day, with more than usual feeling, he spoke

4. This balance was not always kept. When President Prio Socarras was overthrown by Batista, March 10, 1952, the Cuban dollar reserve was $540 million. Seven years later, when Batista escaped, it had shrunk to $70 million.

5. See Chapter 6.

of the corruption of Cuba's politicians, of the confusion of the liberals, of the complete prostration of the workers. Some act of sacrifice, he said, was needed to save Cuba. "I have given all my thought to the huge problem of Cuba's sickness. It has not been enough. Perhaps if I give my life, a miracle will occur." Whereupon, at the microphone, Eduardo Chibas, the honest man, fired a pistol at his temple.

Many a young Cuban, Fidel Castro among them, heard the message of that desperate, hopeful shot. Legal methods of reform, it said to them, will never work: there must be a new matrix for an entire birth. Old violence imprisoned Cuba, only new force can free it. But these were not terrorists, not nihilists. The force they now accepted was the means of a direct contact with the Cuban earth. If they touched Cuba, they would touch the peasants and the workers of Cuba, and in a modern myth of Antaeus,[6] strength would issue: Cuba would at last come to be, after so many centuries of travail.

These young people were not theorists. Doubtless some of them had read the revolutionary literature: Marx, Sorel, Kropotkin. The impulse moving them was more immediate, above all more intimate. In their answer to the sacrificial violence of their dead leader, there was doubtless a mysticism of the body as the flame of spirit. But not explicit, even as the laws of agrarian reform they would soon be writing were not yet explicit. This mysticism was simply the intuition that the human body living on earth is the beginning of cosmic revelation. (These large words were not theirs.) They would bodily withdraw, at the risk of death, from the false Cuba of Batista and the Dollar; they would bodily—again at the risk of death— *live* the embrace with their deep land. And from their simple physical acts with simple peasants, giving them land, receiving from them food, a life would issue which would be Cuba.

This was the lesson of Chibas' death for Fidel Castro and his friends. It reveals the audacity of what they would soon do

6. Antaeus, giant son of Terra and Neptune, received renewed strength from his mother, Earth, each time he was thrown down.

to be spontaneous, questionless, irresistible, like the act of love.

Today the barracks of Cuba have all become schools. Cuba still has an army, but most of it is engaged in public works: the building of roads, swamp drainage, forestation. The army is to be replaced by a people trained to bear defensive arms, in time of need. Violence, which was a master of Cuba's past, is a stage in Cuba's birth, to be transcended as soon as the violence of the surrounding world allows. This is the implicit thought of the young men and women who lead Cuba today: their sole a priori doctrine! Whether this doctrine is right or wrong, whether workable or doomed, we must understand it, in order to know what occurred in Cuba.

The barracks in Santiago, named for General Moncada, a hero of the war of independence against Spain, was a grim spread of masonry painted a dirty yellow. Walls, thick enough for sentinels to move about on them, enclosed a huge grassless parade ground. From the balcony of the main building, facing the Avenida de los Libertadores directly above the chief of three entrance posts, whose gates were always shut and guarded, one looked down on the heart of the city: the cathedral and its park, the public market crowded with peasants and their produce, with braying donkeys and klaxons of cars crawling at donkey pace through the thick human substance. And finally the bay. It is a long curving creature, this bay, shaped like a vast writhing sea worm. Unlike most of Cuba's harbors, which are invading sea, it is landlocked and its contours suggest invasion of the sea by the surrounding mountains. Even in Camaguey which lies at the center of the island, far from both coasts, the sea rules. Not in Santiago, which seems perpetually conscious of its Sierras. Most of the political rebellions in Cuba have had their origin and their heart in the regions of Santiago. The city itself has often been a balance-weight to the more fluid westward provinces. Unlike all the

Cuban cities, except Trinidad, Santiago is perpendicular. Unlike Trinidad, Santiago is forever looking forward.

The grim Moncada Barracks fascinated the young men and women who had learned the lesson Chibas taught in death, but had never learned in life. Some were students in Havana; some had homes in Artemisa, Guanajay, and other provincial towns. Their discussions had been largely theoretical. They had read Marx but were not Marxists. The Spanish predilection for syndicalism was in them but they were nationalists. Their true guide was Jose Marti, the Cuban poet who made act of word. The Moncada fortress overbearing Cuba's most revolutionary city was a symbol of attack for them, as it was a symbol of possession for Fulgencio Batista.

Fidel Castro, twenty-six years old, a practicing lawyer in Havana, appeared before the Supreme Court and, under the 1940 Constitution, which was still technically the law, accused Fulgencio Batista of crimes against the state, for which the minimum sentence would have been one hundred years in prison, the maximum sentence, death. Of course, the court was not ready to arraign the man who sat in the Presidential Palace with the army at hand. And, of course, Castro had not expected otherwise. He had gone through the motions of the law; he had proved the law's impotence; he was ready now, he and his friends, for action.

The plan was to assault the Moncada fortress. From there, if they succeeded, they would occupy the friendly city, and with gathering force repudiate and unseat Batista, proceeding to immediate elections under the 1940 Constitution.

At first, before their preparations warmed them, they were far from sure they would succeed. Since they counted on surprise, the need of absolute secrecy would hold their number down to a maximum of about one hundred and fifty. The Moncada fortress housed eight hundred soldiers fully armed with up-to-date equipment. One of the young men, who did not survive, stated the problem for them all:

We must all go with faith in our victory. But if our destiny is adverse, we must be valiant in defeat; for what happens to us will become known, and our readiness to die for our country will be repeated by all youth of Cuba. Our example will inspire them to sacrifice and will mitigate the sorrow we bring to our parents and other loved ones. To die for the Fatherland is to live!

Soon, the preparations absorbed them; and the more energy they poured into their work, the more certain they became that they would win. They needed funds since they were without exception young and without fortune. A few received a modest allowance from wealthy parents. (This had been the case with Fidel and Raul Castro when they were students.) A few had good jobs. Others had savings. All they could touch or borrow, they emptied into the treasury. Some sold their cars. One, who had received a bonus of $5,000 from General Electric, gave $4,000. Some had expensive photo equipment which they sold. Some pawned their girls' jewels. They raised, according to Fidel Castro's account, exactly $16,480. They bought a small chicken farm four miles from Siboney on the Bay of Santiago, where it meets the sea. They equipped it with the tools of chicken raising and stored away rifles, pistols, sawed-off shotguns, and one machine gun. The farm was their "cover." Already, in the towns they came from—Havana, Artemisa, and others—they had practiced shooting. They borrowed sixteen cars, picked up from several hiding-places on the eve of action. They obtained regulation army uniforms (through the quartermaster-general's office, to which one of the conspirators belonged). Indeed, so complex and so complete were their preparations that $16,000 seems a small sum to have covered their expenses. According to another of the leaders who rode in the first car, Commandante Jesus Montane, the total sum raised was $22,000.

July 25 and 26 are carnival in Santiago, the festival of Santa Ana. The streets teem with visitors and revelers. A few cars coming from the country before dawn, along with those of farmers, will not be noticed. The soldiers in the barracks, after carousing all night, will be sleeping it off. As the time narrowed, another mood possessed the small brigade. They had been filled, first, with a faith that embraced the possibility of failure: faith that their deed was rooted in a value separate from this act's particular result. As they worked in this faith, they became rationally certain (so it appeared to them) that they would not fail, that they could not fail, for they had with them justice and the people. Against them the hirelings of Batista were bound to surrender. So sure of this were the conspirators that they stressed the importance of not using their weapons, of not killing, except in extreme necessity.

Now as time drew in and vanished, and there remained the immediate moment of the act, an unknown joy possessed them: an ecstasy without time and without failure. As they took their places in the cars and assembled the weapons, they felt that whatever occurred must be good, for it was already within them.

They totaled 165, including an unarmed physician. The two women who had run their household at the farm insisted just before the departure on their right to come along. In the mood of joy possessing them all, why not? It was decided that the two women should accompany the men as nurses. Each of the sixteen cars carried uniformed men, one of whom was the leader of the others. The watchword: Do not shoot unless you must.

The four miles to the city were without incident. The road and the deed ahead absorbed each life, which had bestowed itself, and flowered in the peace of self-bestowal. The night grew pale with the dawn coming. Near the Moncada, a detachment of twenty-one men and the two women, led by Abel Santamaria, the brother of one of the women, branched off for the City Hospital, on higher ground just beyond the fortress walls. A second and larger group, captained by Raul, Fidel's younger brother, struck out for the Palace of Justice, also on higher ground, diagonal from the fortress. Their tactical purpose was to establish a cross-fire, if needed, to protect the main invasion led by Fidel Castro.

The first car of his group came up to Post 3: the sentinel saw the sergeant's uniform, saluted and opened the gate; four or five cars followed. They were already deep in the parade ground and the dormitories at their extreme left slumbered. One of the men stepped down from his car, caught his foot and stumbled. His readied revolver fired. At that instant, the roving sentinels on the walls, called the *posta cosaka*, became aware of the invasion. The rebels had been wrongly informed that there would be no watch at this hour. The one shot waked the dormitories. A man rushed out toward the alarm bell. The invaders, remembering their word, "Do not shoot unless you must!" hesitated a half instant and the alarm rang. Now, the man fell—too late. Men raced from their bunks, half-dressed, naked, their rifles already speaking. Even now it might not have been too late, since they were "in"—but seven cars were missing! One had a puncture. The others got lost in the dark circuitous streets of Santiago, and hearing the shots which proved that the surprise had failed, tried to find their way back to Siboney. Raul's assignment to take the Palace of Justice made a perfect score. He helped now to cover the retreat of the main division. But the men whose goal was the hospital were trapped in it: the first prisoners and the first martyrs of what became a revolution.

The assault on Moncada presents a social-psychological problem. These able students and prosperous young businessmen appear to have deliberately purchased death for themselves. Did they truly believe they could overwhelm 800 professional soldiers in a fortified arsenal? And if by chance they had won their first skirmish, what of Batista's 20,000 soldiers in the background?

They did succeed, for the country rang with wonder and admiration. They did meet Batista's army, and they destroyed it. For this, their intelligence and skill, as we shall see, deserve much credit, but not all. Something more was needed for such individual prowess; one is tempted to say, for such magic. This island, its organic health surviving its several violent and vicious pasts—total annihilation of its first dwellers, piracy and war, unnatural exploitation and corruption—has some principle of creativity for survival against stupendous odds, as if the principle lay in the very odds against it.

5. Sugar against Tobacco

SUGAR was the first modern industry of the Antilles. It was run by power, and the cheapest form of power was the African slave. Slaves themselves became a commodity, sold for profit. And the profit was so great that many a sugar *central* had paid for its capital investment within a year of its construction. The entire process of mass production of sugar lent itself from the outset to factory methods. No individual *made* sugar, as no individual *makes* a motor car. There were men with separate tasks, as along an assembly line: furnace man, grinder, handler of the *guarape,* alkalizer, machinist, hand for filter and *tacho* —as there were men to plant (a single stalk without human help might yield harvest for as long as forty years), to cut, and to load into the nearest port by train or cart. The work was collective; the skill needed was minimal; and the result was a sum of sweetness sold by the ton, a mere anonymous abstraction.

Sugar had been imported into Cuba, to which it was not native. Its route seems to have been India, Arabia, Egypt, and the Mediterranean coasts; and the Atlantic coast from the Antilles to Brazilian Bahia. Columbus brought it with him in 1493, not dreaming of its immense ramifications. It fitted perfectly the mood of early mercantile capitalism; the slave could be caught as passively as coal is mined, and sold at huge profit. It also fitted, through the slave trade, the fiendishness of the pirates. It fed the dawning European will for power, solving problems of production, mechanics and waste, expressing all the nascent talent of the European for appropriating natural forces to his own uses and aggrandizement. It called for capital. The product was an impersonal as gold—and far more useful.

Think of the elements that went into an up-to-date sugar mill in Cuba: the bank and the stockholders that financed the plant and speculated on the harvest, the large landownership required for mass production, the machinery, the impersonal use of labor enslaved or imported for seasonal work, the absenteeism which the whole process encouraged through the need of share investment. Such elements summed to capitalist enterprise. Yet capitalism is not within the ethos of Spain, which slowed the process in Cuba with its large feudal estates perforated by thousands of small holdings. Spain still ruled, with the personalism of its culture. But sugar is impersonal. The owner of even the humblest cane field or *trapiche* will not be able to recognize his product, that abstract commodity of sugar, once it has been posted in the world market. In accord with capitalist process, however alien to Spain's ethos, the number of small and independent sugar works was continuously shrinking. Before Spain left Cuba, thousands of *centrales* had vanished. Individual owners could not build themselves railroads to port or compete with the rates and rebates of the large producers. They were forced to sell out. In 1959, 182 sugar factories, predominantly American, owned most of the good ground of Cuba. The Americans alone had 1.9 million acres.

Fernando Ortiz, outstanding cultural scholar of Cuba, has written a book (1940) entitled *Cuban Counterpoint of Sugar and Tobacco,* which is a masterpiece. More than one of the American nations has produced a volume that incarnates the spirit of its people. Such is Mark Twain's *Huckleberry Finn,* the saga of a boy floating with the current of a continental river, as the immature American people has floated down with its current; such is *Os Sertaōs* of Brazil, *Martin Fierro* of Argentina—and the great playful essay of Ortiz. He says, "Tobacco and Sugar are the most important characters in the history of Cuba," and he writes the searching contrapuntal dialogue of

Don Tobaco and Dona Azucar. But if the title of Dona is granted only to a gentlewoman, I must dissent from sugar's being thus sexed and honored. Sugar is a woman only as a whore is a woman. Sugar is a cold, impersonal bawd selling the pleasure of her body without personal touch, without love, at a price ruled by world quotas.

But tobacco! Here is the dark flesh, the warm, silken flesh of individual response: the delight, the venom, the inexorable doom in smoke, of human intercourse! The Indians, of course, made a ritual of the use of tobacco, which they never cheapened into the compulsive tic of the modern world, which lacks even the dignity of the question how the habit grew and what it means. The cutting of the leaf, permitted only by the dark of the moon and by torchlight, and the intake through the mouth of the aroma in which both earth and death by burning are incarnate, were ritual to the native, as distinct from our dull smoke-bondage as religion is from neurosis. But one may still sense the charisma in the color and smell of the ripe fields and the shorn fields, and in the thatch-roofed storehouses, hermetically sealed, of Cuba's tobacco treasure.

In Cuba free men, not slaves, have conducted the delicate upbringing of tobacco. From the selecting and placing of the seed in the coldframe to the exquisitely hazardous transplanting; from the nursing of the *mata* (the stem) to the careful cutting, "burning" and curing of the leaf, and on to the classification of the product into sixteen distinct categories, the precious growth has been in the agile, subtle hands of men and women whose touch made an exchange with the leaf—with the *centro-fino* from the middle of the *mata*, silken and strong, best for the wrapper; or with the precocious new leaves after the first cutting, which give personality to every harvest. Such is the finesse of the operation that certain leaves must be warmed only by the heat of the earth on which they are placed like babes on the breast of the mother. When a year of sparse rain comes, and modern systems of spray and irrigation must be substituted for the gentle natural process, the result, despite all science, is a leaf inferior in savor.

Tobacco could be degraded to a slave-labor factory for mass production. Virginia and the Carolinas were examples. But even the cigar factory of today's Cuba stresses the individual. In the long, dark-brown room, redolent of leaf, sit perhaps four hundred men and women, each at a little table with a hardwood plate and and a semicircular steel blade for cutting and fitting. There may be a few mechanical gadgets: tubes for size, scissors to snip off too-long residues, molds for different shapes. But the sense of the room is the sense of the individual worker whose hands move like a pianist's playing a soft nocturne. By an old tradition, each room has a reader; he usually reads the news in the mornings, and in the afternoons a book selected by popular vote. Today, he speaks through an amplifier: a concession to the times, and not a happy one, for the electronics denature the human voice, which used to merge with the quick fingers and the leaf's aroma. On another floor of the old house, cigars are being manufactured by machines, complicated and ingenious apparatuses. The worker presses down the leaf, the machine takes it, cuts it, fills it, evens its size and after a dozen automatic precision operations rolls it down to the hands of another worker, who applies a gummy tip—and the cigar is ready to go up in smoke. But not yet quite ready to be sold. In upper regions, the workers place bands on the cigars, make handsome cedar boxes with fragile sheets of wood between the layers, apply labels and covers, and finally pack the cigars, which are now ready for the great world markets, each of which—the United States, Britain, Germany—has its preferred shapes, colors (from olive-green to brown) and strengths of flavor.

The cigar factories of Florida, Philadelphia and New York, in which the workers were predominantly Cuban, financed (as we have seen) Marti's schemes and plans for invading and freeing Cuba. The cigar-maker (*torcidor*) was a meditative man and the institution of factory reader often made him a radical with anarchist-syndicalist predilections. And the cigar itself never quite lost its ritual past. If it had no other ritual aspect, it was expensive until quite recently, and without reading Veblen the upper classes knew the uses of extravagance. In seventeenth-century England, a pound of tobacco was worth the equivalent of $120. Not until the cigarette[1] exhaled a nervous cloud over the whole world was tobacco vulgarized. Ortiz treats the cigarette with contempt. "The cigarette . . . dwarfish, feeble, beggarly, without inside or outside guts, full of tobacco wastage without purity and wearing a miserable shirt of paper." He blames the cigarette vogue on our latter day stage of capitalism. It is a diddering smoke, he writes, cheap and quick and tasteless: an abstract "smoke" almost like the abstract "sweet" of sugar.

By the end of the eighteenth century, the Havana *tobaco* (as the Cubans call their cigar) was conquering Europe's and North America's upper classes, and the values of these classes were prevailing over the mystery in tobacco. Nevertheless, the mystery is there. The poorest Cuban, with a *tobaco* tilted up from his chin, which he has "twisted" for himself from discarded leaves in the bin of his town's factory, partakes of this mystery: the tasteless, colorless and deadly poison in the aroma. And I suspect that the millionaire partakes of the same mystery, although he knows nothing of it. More than the leaf is going up in smoke: the capitalist culture is upon the funeral pyre. In the first stages, when the tobacco was smoked *pure* (the *puro* cigar and the pipe), the touch of death was concealed within a rich and eloquent mist. Then, in the cigarette, the richness vanished: the residue was the tasteless, colorless poison.

In the contest between tobacco and sugar, between the deeply personal and the shallowly impersonal, anonymous, abstract: sugar is winning.

1. Spain invented the *cigarro* (cigarette) in the seventeenth century. It was supposed to resemble a certain locust, *cigarra*, in the Andalusian countryside and hence its name.

6. *Blood and Irony: Cuban-U.S. Relations*

ALREADY in 1809, Thomas Jefferson was writing: "We must have the Floridas and Cuba." In 1823 he added: "I have ever looked on Cuba as the most interesting addition which could be made to our system of states. . . . Her addition to our Confederacy is exactly what is wanting to advance our power as a nation to the point of its utmost interest. . . ." The same year President John Quincy Adams ponderously and forebodingly declared:

> Such indeed are, between the interests of that island and of this country, the geographical, commercial, moral and political relations, formed by nature, gathering in the process of time and even now verging to maturity, that in looking forward to the probable course of events, for the short period of half a century, it is scarcely possible to resist the conviction that the annexation of Cuba to our federal republic will be indispensable to the continuance and integrity of the union itself.

It was Adams who made the poetic metaphor of Cuba: the fruit which when ripe would drop from Spain's tree into our lap. And already before Jefferson, Benjamin Franklin had looked with lusty appetite on Cuba. Hardly an American statesman (not to mention the jingo politicians) of the period before our Civil War failed to register his confidence in the American destiny of Cuba; James Madison, Henry Clay, John C. Calhoun, Daniel Webster among them. And it is an open secret that the Monroe Doctrine, ostensibly aimed against the American designs of the Holy Alliance, was really aimed at Britain, which had a steadfast eye on Cuba. Cuba, our policy agreed, must remain Spain's until it fell to us. Bolivar knew and feared this. C. Chapman, in his *History of the Cuban Republic*, writes: ". . . it was the Cuban question that caused the United States to delay in sending delegates to Bolivar's Panama Congress of 1826. When at length they were allowed to start they received instructions that were opposed to the separation of Cuba from Spain." Henry Clay's official note of December 10, 1825, virtually warned Bolivar to keep hands off Cuba, despite its being an integral part of America Hispana. (Free Colombia and Mexico had already planned a joint invasion. Cuba itself was filled with underground clubs and Masonic orders designed for action similar to that of Venezuela.)

All this happened, not because the Americans were villains. Jefferson, archetype of the American statesman, was convinced that admission to our system would be an inestimable benefit to the Cubans, many of whose best men openly advocated annexation. If this was "imperialism," as most Cuban historians insist, it had a cultural dimension. Jefferson would have approved of the small Cuban farms, so distinct from the huge *latifundios* of Mexico and Peru. His own America, he hoped, was to be a land of free small farmers, craftsmen and mechanics, in a loose union of quasi-independent states. Why should not Cuba join it? The impossibility of this Utopia in a machine age whose mass production compelled centralized power escaped Jefferson. He was all wrong in his economics, in his sociology, in his hope of a state that "governed little." He knew little about the Cubans or, for that matter, about America Hispana. This was his "crime," if any. Indeed, shortly before he died, when he already knew the abyss between his fantasied "commune" of free men and the new slavocracy of the new iron monsters, which capitalism was forging into an expansive imperialism of its own, he expressed his doubt about Cuba. "Hands off!" he said at last, seeing what Emerson expressed a little later: "the Thing is in the saddle." But no one heard him.

Later President-politicians—Pierce, Polk, Buchanan—preferred a plan to get Cuba by purchase. Offers were made to

Spain, were haughtily rejected. As the United States grew stronger, the possibility of a war was again favored. (This, remember, was the time of the Mexican War and of the ambition of the Slave South to expand its political control.) Franklin Pierce put it baldly: "If Spain persists in her refusal to sell, we'll take the island." This was amended to the proposition that Spain be compelled to grant Cuba independence, with the United States, which had helped to free Cuba, as "favored nation." (A conjunction of these two methods was, of course, what took place: the United States helped to free Cuba from Spain and by means of the Platt Amendment to the Cuban constitution made Cuba an American protectorate, an American "plantation.")[1]

Meanwhile, the ironic paradox prevailed: the first of the American republics, founded on liberty and dedicated to its spread throughout the hemisphere, became the protector of archaic Spain's ever more desperate will to hold on to Cuba. Irony, we have seen, is an old story in Cuba. Cuba failed to produce gold and was virtually abandoned by the first settlers, who rushed to Mexico and Peru. It was unsafe because of the ravaging pirates. As a site of sugar monoculture it could not compare with Haiti, Santo Domingo or Barbados. Ferocious but competent governors, such as Francisco Vives, kept the peace with the garrote and exile. In the years before and after Bolivar's doomed Congress of Panama (its goal was a hemisphere of united nations, without slaves and pledged to solve their American problems without war), Cuba bristled with attempts of revolution. Expeditions started from Mexico, Colombia, New York, and were crushed with the aid of Washington.

1. Article III of the Amendment, voted by Congress and forced, as we shall see, upon the Cuban people, reads: "The Government of Cuba consents that the United States may exercise the right to intervene for the preservation of Cuban independence, the maintenance of a government adequate for the protection of life, property and individual liberty, and for discharging the obligations with respect to Cuba imposed by the Treaty of Paris on the United States, now to be assumed and undertaken by the Government of Cuba."

The young Hispanic countries were far too weak to antagonize the United States. A Cuban delegation almost convinced President Monroe that the way to win Cuba was through independence (the course of Texas). Cuba at once became involved in American politics, and it was the political freedom of our country which blocked the freedom of Cuba. Irony, but Cuba was learning to suffer and to be alone.

The underpopulated island meanwhile produced intellectuals of remarkable stature: the priest Felix Varela (1788–1853), who in New York edited *El Habañero,* a journal dedicated to Cuban independence; liberal landowners, such as Jose Antonio Saco, and Jose de la Luz Caballero, the educator; the great poets Placido[2] and Heredia (the former garroted, the latter exiled). Wistfully they looked toward the United States. In its war of independence against England, it had the help of the French navy and of Spain also, helping with money and supplies, if not with fighters. Now the Cubans pleaded: "If any nation would come forward and offer us protection!" No one came forward. Spain, stripped of most of its empire, sent huge armies against little Cuba: larger ones than faced San Martin and Bolivar with a continent behind them.

The Cubans went forward. They lobbied in Washington. Narciso Lopez, by birth a Venezuelan, raised ships and a polyglot army in New York, landed in Cardenas, east of Havana, in 1850, and died, garroted. There were Negro rebellions, which complicated the scene with the fear of slave uprisings, as in Haiti. But race war could not thrive in Cuba, where the colored were never a majority as in the British and French islands. For two centuries, the island was tortured almost without a pause by Spain's Caribbean wars with England, Holland and France. Peace treaties were broken before the ink on them was dry. The long shores and snug harbors of Cuba were opened to endless raids, until the distinction blurred between piracy and legal conflict. Already in the eighteenth century, the American colonies of Britain had taken a hand in

2. His real name was Gabriel de la Concepcion Valdes.

the turmoil of Cuba. In Vernon's Raid (1741), an army of 600 men from New England, New York, Pennsylvania and Virginia, landed near Guantanamo (as the Americans were to land in 1898) and sacked Santiago. The British conquest of Havana (1762) was the work of 60 warships and 22,000 men, *one-fourth* of whom were Americans, not British. Cuba suffered, but was forced to hold its suffering inward, where it fermented character: violence and patience, the sense of inferiority and self-value.

W. C. C. Claiborne, Louisiana's first territorial governor, had written to Jefferson: "Cuba is the real mouth of the Mississippi, and the nation possessing it may possibly at a future day command the Western country. But let the island be ours and the American union is placed beyond the reach of change." So Jefferson bought Louisiana.

An American journalist, John Louis O'Sullivan, editor of *The Democratic Review,* invented the slogan "Manifest Destiny," and the American statesmen believed it and made it their own, pursuing and rationalizing American expansion. But as invisibly and subtly as the winds bearing seed, Cuba that knew little of Jefferson began to oppose him and to sense its own destiny in its own shape and terms.

Cuba was weak—and somehow strong; Cuba was minor—and somehow major. In the nineteenth century, the Cuban poets (for the most part in exile) began to speak like prophets.

Cuba began to prosper. It suffered but it prospered, and pain suffused and became part of its thriving. There were few slaves, and agriculture was diverse: sugar, tobacco, coffee, livestock. The population grew, and was Cuban. Unlike later on, when Spain clutched fearfully at power, Cubans held many offices of importance.

In 1868 came open war against the mother country. It was led at first by the landowners, who differed among themselves in aim: some were for independence, some for autonomy under Spain, some for annexation to the United States. Officially, the war lasted ten years, and failed. Really, it became transformed into a popular war of all the people and lasted thirty years. The first President was Carlos Manuel de Cespedes (1819–1874), a lawyer, teacher and aristocrat, who was not trusted by the delegates who chose him. They pushed him out; and the Spaniards, when they came to arrest him and he resisted, shot him. The Pact of Zanjon (1878) was supposed to be a treaty of peace, making concessions of autonomy and representation in the Cortes of Madrid. The promises were cynically ignored.

When the war began, Grant was President of the United States. Grant was a good man and a great soldier; but he knew little about politics. He trusted his friends—who robbed the national till. He sympathized with the Cuban revolutionists and with his own hand wrote out a proclamation supporting their cause by granting them belligerency rights to import needed instruments of war. Before he could sign it, Secretary of State Hamilton Fish gave the President a lesson in the "facts of life" concerning Cuba. The proclamation was never issued; the old policy of reinforcing Spain in Cuba, until the ripe fruit fell, continued.

American aid to Cuba, credits to buy arms and to build ships, might have sufficed to break Spain's desperate grasp. Cuba in peace could easily have paid its debt. The man who officially prevented this excellent business transaction was the soldier who had done most to save the American Union. The irony continued.

In *The Rediscovery of Man*[3] I showed how the Reformation, the conquest of global frontiers, capitalism and nationalism variously issued from the unmaking of the Catholic synthesis of Europe. Roman theology, through its concept of the immortality of the individual soul, had aggrandized the ego. In theory, and in the practice of the Saints, God's presence within the soul transfigured the ravening, free-roving ego. But without adequate psychology and method the contrary occurred: the

3. By Waldo Frank (New York: Braziller, 1958).

individual ego and the ego of the collectivity were exalted and hugely enhanced. The results were what we call both good and evil: "good," the conquest of nature by science, bequeathed to man's possessive will by God; "evil," the expansions of lust and greed in a new capitalist class and in the breeding of irresponsible magnates; "evil," the newly aggressive and anarchic nations; good," their contributions to a broader if not deeper culture; "good," the enterprise of pioneer and settler; "evil," their enslavement of defenseless races in other continents and of defenseless classes (and these classes' children) at home; "evil," the pirates who for three centuries raped the fair islands of the Caribbean; "good," the businessmen and the technologists who "spread" modern civilization.

The Big Business magnates ranged in variety from a Henry Ford, who remained at home and took advantage less of labor than of a continental situation, and a John D. Rockefeller, who organized the satisfaction of a continental need by piratical methods, to a J. P. Morgan, who organized the conquests of other magnates, and a Cecil Rhodes, who, like his Dutch, French and American equivalents, took advantage of superior skills to enslave whole populations. The kinship of Big Business and piracy had already been revealed in the fact that Elizabeth, Queen of England, with many another aristocrat, held shares in a slave-trade corporation.

The variety of the pirates rivaled the variety of the magnates; and often they converged. Henry Morgan, whose father was a Protestant pastor, was knighted and became a member of Parliament (already in large part a bourgeois body); Drake, also knighted, organized his loot of land and treasure, like Bartholomew Roberts, who established a counterpolice on the high seas. His men had to obey ascetic orders about food and drink and their leader appeared before them only in the full-dress uniform of an officer of the navy. Francis L'Ollonnais went to battle in a fop's clothes and shared his winnings for years with Sir Thomas Modiford, governor of Barbados. In 1583 the French corsairs did battle with the Spaniards for five days in the Carribbean. At night they exchanged dinner invitations, rivaling one another in the choice wines and game they offered to their guests—and at dawn resumed their bloody battle. Edward Teach, called "Blackbeard," was a sadist who loved, when he got ashore, to mask his butcheries in pagan frolics. Captain William Kidd was a sober, somewhat sullen sailor who loved the kiss of money. He became the fighting arm of a group of London businessmen, and when he attended their directors' meetings he had to wash the blood from his hands, lest the stain be seen by his churchgoing partners. Captain Avery was a romantic; a play about him, called *The Successful Pirate,* ran in London while he was there to see it. He loved diamonds and turned his loot into the glittering stones. He hoped to settle in New England, but diamonds were not currency in Boston; the city was too reticent for his need of publicity and he returned to England.

It is estimated that in the eighteenth century 10,000 pirates operated in the Caribbean. The Isle of Pines, south of Cuba, was their home, and they had another in Nassau (New Providence), where the ex-pirate Woodes Rogers, once governor of Barbados, had set up a community in which the buccaneers "could rest, settle, or recuperate their strength for new sallies." "From Rags to Riches" was the motto of Charles Vane, borrowed by many another cutter-of-throats-for-gain, and finally the watchword of the rising business order.

The prototype of both species, buccaneer and magnate, was perhaps Columbus. He sailed across the sea, convinced that the True Faith and the best social order went along with him; and this conviction won him credit with both monks and queen to outfit his caravels in Spain. What he found, he blandly assumed to be his, pressing his right, and his heirs' right to it, forever. By intelligence and method, he far surpassed the pirates, perhaps also in greed. (The abler pirates also justified their depredations by linking them to a national flag and to the "true religion".) And like the later magnates who enslaved an entire race in Africa, subjugated entire provinces in Asia, or set up states within states in Mexico's oil fields, in the copper lands of north Chile, in the company towns of the nineteenth-century United States, Columbus was certain that he brought blessings with him.

It is within this perspective that Cuba's revolution must be understood, and above all by the Cubans and by the Cubans' leaders. Events as disparate as the voyages of Columbus, the ravages of pirate and slaver, the positivist philosophies of empiricism, the rise of the political democracies and their economic exploitations, the victories of abstract science—all these events whose structures, social and aesthetic, *leave the whole man out*—must be related together as processes within the culture of capitalism. But superficial reactions against this culture, such as the orthodox dialectical materialism of Russia and China, also leave the whole man out; are also *within* that deficient culture. The Cuban birth is important because its *deed* appears to embrace and even already to express the whole man. Unlike more routine communism, it does not attack the culture of capitalism by reciting the dogmatic values of that very culture.

Cuba is a small country; all that it has been able to do is but a promise, fraught—as we shall see—with dangers. But if the promise lives it will grow, it will variate, and it could make valid—as we shall also see—the hemisphere myth of a new world.

If the promise is allowed to live . . . !

7. *The Betrayed Republics: U.S.A. and Cuba*

I

THE chief adversary of Marti's revolution and its ideals was a man, perhaps unknown to Marti even by name, who certainly had never heard of Marti[1]—William McKinley, born at Niles, Ohio, and in the year after Marti's death President-elect of the United States. Grover Cleveland, whom he succeeded, had been under public pressure to intervene in Cuba, after newspapers and business forces played up the carnage and the starving children for ends of their own. Cleveland resisted: war would mean more soldiers' pensions, which would mean more taxes, and it was Cleveland's first duty, as he saw it, to keep taxes down, not to clean up the backyard of a disorderly neighbor.

McKinley was of a different substance. He was a religious man. Each night and morning, on his knees, he prayed for guidance in the decisions before him. He was a loyal man: loyal to his invalid wife, loyal to his friends who had exalted him to his high office (among them an ambitious magnate, Mark Hanna), loyal above all to his people who, he was personally sure, had the Truth as no other of God's children had it. In his way, McKinley was as *devoted* a man as Marti, and in his private life a good deal saintlier, by common standards.

The chief difference between them lay in the totalities of their respective visions. Marti saw man whole; saw a continent of humble humans, most of them ignorant, hungry, yet in each the potential of God revealed through love and beauty. McKin-

---

1. The *Encyclopaedia Britannica* contains no biography of Marti, even today.

ley's sense of a continent, its peoples and their potential, was a dim background; his sight did not go so far. Yet he was not "nearsighted," since his close vision of man and men was also blurred. He saw the churches of his hometown, that had the ticket to Heaven; he saw the businessmen who had the ticket for the workingman's "full dinner pail," and who had backed him whenever he ran for office. His sense of stewardship came right out of the New Testament, the Parable of the Talents, with no reference to such wild and radical speech as the Sermon on the Mount. Early in his career, campaigning for the sound gold dollar, he had said: "We cannot gamble with anything so sacred as money."

He believed in the United States' imperial destiny of control over all America, no less than such good lieutenants as young Theodore Roosevelt (who, looking ahead, had sent Commodore Dewey to the Pacific with orders to be "ready when war came," and it was coming) and Secretary of the Navy Long, whose words could have been his own, hailing the day not of "any mere selfish *imperial* dominion" but of "the *imperial* moral and physical expansion of all the peoples, *under* the broad shield of the United States of America." That day was already present in the eyes of William McKinley. It meant obedience to the people's wish that Spain get out of Cuba; and it meant no less that American business interests, which had built up their glorious country, should not lose by the transaction.

In 1898 events became precipitate in Cuba as if history, after a century's delay, were suddenly in a hurry. Weyler had been recalled, more in deference to American than to Spanish public opinion. The queen-regent had made it very clear, through diplomatic circles, that Spain was ready peacefully to dispose of Cuba, provided the dignity of the crepuscular empire be saved and Spanish economic interests honored—as they would best be under the flag of the United States.

The battleship *Maine* sailed into Havana Harbor on a friendly call to a friendly nation, and Spain's cruiser, *Vizcaya*, returned the visit to New York. On February 16 the *Maine* exploded with the loss of over two hundred fifty lives: mostly sailors, for the officers were being festive in the city. The condolences of the Spanish authorities were profuse. But the press and the press-aroused American people had the pretext for open hostility they wanted.

The wave for war became tidal. Sincerely and consciously moved by the starved *reconcentrados,* the good citizens had wanted Spain *out* of Cuba. Now it was to become evident that less consciously they wanted their own country *in.* The magnates and the imperialists, the family of the Mark Hannas, the Theodore Roosevelts, the W. B. Hearsts, knew this consciously. And knew that only a victorious war could achieve what they wanted. This was, primarily, a free hand in all Spain's residual domain, not only Cuba but Puerto Rico and the Philippines as well. Roosevelt, the most articulate of his kind, specifically wanted *battle* and the kind of imperial prestige only battle could bring. And he intended to be in it. But the people resisted this expansive egoism within themselves (witness the Populists and the silverites led by William Jennings Bryan.) The people felt guilty about it. And compensated for their sense of guilt by insisting not only that Spain leave Cuba but that Cuba be free, that Cuba's insurgent government be recognized, and that the United States disavow all claims on Cuba, once Cuba had been freed.

The people's immediate voice and will were in the Congress. On April 19, after much wrangling, the two Houses—the Representatives by a huge majority, the Senate by a more moderate one—passed a Joint Resolution:

Resolved, by the Senate and House of Representatives in Congress assembled.

First. That the people of the island of Cuba are, and of right ought to be, free and independent.

Second. That it is the duty of the United States to demand, and the government of the United States does hereby demand, that the government of Spain at once relinquish its authority and government in the island of Cuba and withdraw its land and naval forces from Cuba and Cuban waters.

Third. That the President of the United States, be, and he hereby is, directed and empowered to use the entire land and naval forces of the United States, and to call into the actual service of the United States the militia of the several States to such extent as may be necessary to carry these resolutions into effect.

To this was added and passed what is known as the Teller Amendment:

That the United States hereby disclaims any disposition or intention to exercise sovereignty, jurisdiction or control over said island, except for the pacification thereof, and asserts its intention, when that has been accomplished, to leave government and control of the island to its people.

This was war. But equally important: the recognition of the actual revolutionary government in Cuba as "the true lawful government of that island"—originally passed by the Congress —was avoided.

This was the work of President McKinley, whose ambiguities were so typical of his people's nature as to make him in his way a prophet. This refusal to recognize the republic which already existed in Cuba freed the American government to do what it chose to do, in Cuba.

McKinley believed in the Cubans' right to liberty; and no less in the right of American business—the living anatomy and organs of the country—to do what it wanted to do in Cuba. What it wanted, of course, was to make money: a great and unrestricted deal of money. The convictions incarnate in McKinley summed to ambiguity and to the hypocrisy of trying to rationalize, justify and preserve the contradictions. They characterize the American state policy toward Cuba from that day forward. The American masterpiece was yet to come: the Platt Amendment to the Cuban Constitution, by which the U.S. with its right hand bestowed freedom on Cuba and with its left hand abolished freedom; each hand complacently aware of its own virtue and rights—and of the other's.

Marti responded to all the values and cultural substances of his America by integrating them into a single grandiose conception, more religious than political, which refused all active contradiction: the organic instrument outlined in the Manifesto of Monte Cristi. McKinley responded to the values of his hometown, both humanitarian and commercial, both vaporous and concrete, by keeping them separate and ignoring their intrinsic contradictions.

II

The American ambiguity is nowhere more visible than in the Battle of Santiago, which with Dewey's destruction of the Spanish fleet in Manila Bay on May 1, virtually ended the war and with it Spain's American and Asiatic empire, on which, three centuries before, the sun never set. To the American soldiers the Cubans were "niggers," and they disdained them, their rags and their obsolete arms. The Spaniards were the enemy, of course; but they were white, and when they were captured the Americans lavished courtesies upon them to stress their difference from the "mongrel" Cubans for whose freedom they were supposedly at war. Strict instructions from Washington warned the army against any act from which recognition of the present Cuban government might be construed. American officers translated this into justification of surliness and exclusion which at times came to insult.

Particularly guilty of this contemptuous conduct was General Shafter, whose immensely obese body, weighing three hundred pounds, supported a head with nothing in it. Men such as Lieutenant Colonel Leonard Wood and Lieutenant Colonel Theodore Roosevelt were too cultivated to disclose their minds in their conduct. Their letters reveal that they despised the "brown races" of America Hispana, and were certain that the show of granting Cuban independence must lead to annexation.

From the ranks to the top, contradictions reigned in the minds of the liberators of Cuba; which may explain their failure to give the Cubans their due in the victory over Spain. Every year, in the United States, millions of school children study this battle and this war, hardly realizing that there were any Cubans in it! The Cubans at best lurk like ghosts in a nebulous background of events. This makes American misconduct toward them less blameworthy. Can one insult a ghost? Isn't it proper to ignore a ghost, since manifestly ghosts do not exist?

The part of Cuba in the Battle of Santiago, far from being negligible, as our textbooks have it, was crucial and essential. Shafter's strategic plan had been to make a mass assault on Santiago's Morro Castle at the end of the long bay leading to the city. He wanted to land his army of about 15,000 at Aserradero, a tiny port west of the land-locked harbor, cross the jungles of the mountains of the Sierra Maestra, and advance up the open bay northward to the city. General Garcia told him that this route was suicide. The Americans would not get through the jungle. And if, by miracle, they did, the guns of the fort and the fleet would rake and strip them into ribbons. Garcia advised Shafter to land at Daiquiri, east of the city, where his Cuban troops would cover the Americans, and to ascend to El Caney and San Juan Hill, whence the army from the north could spread their wings to enclose the city on its three land sides. Shafter and his staff had the sense to listen and comply. The landing was a success. With great fortitude—despite the bad leadership of the American officers, whose exposed men were torn by Spanish fire and sent up with no artillery support —the Americans stormed El Caney and San Juan (a Negro regiment played a brave part). And a troop of 5,000 Cubans barred the advance from Holguin, northwest of Santiago, of the main Spanish body in the province. At the same time, admirably maneuvring, the Cubans completed the encirclement of Santiago city.

If the Cubans provided the strategy of the battle, and helped to carry it out, they can scarcely be said to have played no part in it. Yet they were not invited to the conferences of the commanders, which closed with the Spaniards' unconditional surrender. And Cuban troops with arms were not admitted to enter the liberated city! (It is only just to add that later on, General Nelson A. Miles, Shafter's superior, apologized to the Cubans for this insult.)

The sequel had no ambiguity. Spain was gone; order began. American mobilization for war had been incompetent and corrupt to the extreme of scandal. Soldiers in uniforms fit for Alaska were sent into the tropics' fiery heat, and fed on spoiled canned food ("embalmed beef," General Miles called it). Guns were shipped with improper ammunition or none at all. Transport vessels sailed from Tampa empty, while others, crammed with sweating soldiers, sweltered for days at anchor. Typhoid, yellow fever, malaria and the heat killed more Americans than Spanish guns. But when, after the armistice, the United States took Cuba in hand, efficiency and sanitation became the rule. The island was not conveyed to its native government, as the Congress Resolutions had promised. It was handled as enemy territory legitimately conquered. But it was scrubbed and put in order by courteous and competent victors.

The Americans had come down to Cuba—the leaders, with an unacknowledged purpose: to possess it. They did possess Cuba, as solidly as Texas, although in other terms, due to distinct conditions. They felt a guilt in this, for Congress had given its word. This guilt moved them to exaggerate what they had done in freeing Cuba and were doing for Cuba; to minimize what the Cubans had done for themselves; but above all to justify their staying on. Witness Leonard Wood's exaggerated reports in his letters to Roosevelt about the filth in the cities, his emphasized conviction that if the army left the filth would return, and his plea that infected Cuba would be a menace to the southern ports of the United States.

Wood built schools. He repaired bridges and broadened roads. He was convinced that Cuba, thankful for such blessings, would eventually ask for annexation; and the vast majority of American officers and politicians agreed. Like many another beneficent proconsul, Wood was deluded, because he lacked true touch with the conquered country. The Cubans were thankful for the sanitation works, needed after the decades of neglect, but they wanted to be free. They were thankful for the last-hour help they had received, but after thirty years of war they wanted a first-hour chance to be themselves.

The Cuban army had not yet been disbanded nor the men sent back to their humble homes. Wood invited Generalissimo Gomez and a small group of Cuban leaders to a day's picnic sail on his yacht. While the daiquiris glittered cold, he assured Gomez that the President meant to honor absolutely the promises of Congress. Moreover, McKinley had a balance of $3 million from the war budget voted by Congress, with which he was ready to pay a $75 bonus to every Cuban veteran, with one proviso: that the army dissolve. Gomez believed Wood, and accepted. When the Platt Amendment was divulged, the Cubans were desperate with anger—at first directed against Gomez, and with impotence. They now had no army. And they knew that the American army would not leave unless and until the American terms were accepted. They knew, moreover, that the American leaders were far from eager to have their army go. They knew that the authorities, headed by Governor Wood, were hoping the Cubans would repudiate the Platt Amendment. Then the American army could stay indefinitely.

The amendment to the Cuban Constitution began by declaring itself to be *"in fulfillment* of the joint resolution of the Congress" which promised independence to Cuba and the withdrawal of American forces from Cuba. It went on to demand:

First. That the government of Cuba shall never enter into any treaty or other compact with any foreign power or powers which will impair or tend to impair the independence of Cuba. . . .

Second. That the said government shall not assume or contract any public debts . . . for the ultimate discharge of which the ordinary revenues of the island . . . shall be inadequate.

Third. That the government of Cuba consents that the United States may exercise the right to intervene for the preservation of Cuban independence, for the maintenance of a government adequate for the protection of life, property and individual liberty and for discharging obligations. . . .

Fourth. That all acts of the United States in Cuba during its military occupancy thereof are ratified and validated. . . .

Fifth. (Refers to sanitation of the Cuban cities.)

Sixth. (Refers to the Isle of Pines.)

Seventh. That to enable the United States to maintain the independence of Cuba and to protect the people thereof, as well as for its own defense, the government of Cuba will sell or lease to the United States lands necessary for coaling or naval stations (Guantanamo). . . .

The Cubans, of course, understood the document to be the definite denial of their independence, and so declared. But from Washington to General Wood came the interpretation of the Word by Elihu Root, McKinley's new Secretary of War:

You are authorized to state officially that in the view of the President the intervention described in the third clause of the Platt Amendment is not synonymous with intermeddling or interfering with the affairs of the Cuban government. . . .

Even now, the Cubans were not convinced by the word magic. Intervention and dependency upon the United States at any moment or upon any pretext judged "necessary" by the United States—the United States *alone*—did not smell sweet to the Cubans, even when it was *not* called "intermeddling and interference."

Garcia and three other Cubans went to Washington to plead with McKinley. He received them courteously but *unofficially,* careful not to let the interview imply the recognition of any government in Cuba. They got nothing. (Garcia took sick and died in New York on the way back.) Everybody knew that the alternative to acceptance meant the continued indefinite occupation of the island. On March 2, 1902, the Convention placed the Platt Amendment, word for word, as ordered, in the new Constitution. The vote was close. Those who with sick heart supported the inclusion, as the lesser of two evils, were among the clearest heads in Cuba.

Cuba had been betrayed by its rescuers and defenders. But *the people* of the United States had also been betrayed. Their emotion and will, voiced in the Congress, had unqualifiedly declared the Cubans' right to unqualified freedom. This emotion and will had energized the American intervention, which then had been exploited to cheat the popular will of both republics.

In 1934 the well-intentioned President Franklin Delano Roosevelt canceled the Platt Amendment (but kept the naval base at Guantanamo). If a substance is poured into a mold and hardens, the mold can be removed and the substance retains its shape. The Platt Amendment was no longer necessary; the dependence of Cuba on the United States was by then a structural fact which only a blow against the structure itself could shatter.

III

The story of Cuba's republic in its first fifty years is not a pretty one. Its foundation of betrayal called for men ready to traffic in and to collaborate with betrayal. Honest servants cannot work well with dishonest material and for a dishonest master. The vice of Havana's tourist industries was the mere façade of a corruption that rotted the legislature and the courts. The American Embassy was the true capitol of Cuba, and the lie of independence which covered this fact was more corrosive even than the fact.

Nevertheless, from its beginning, Cuba's republic had gallant public servants who tried to work in it, despite and within its matrix-lie. Such a man was Enrique Jose Varona, a soldier of seventeen in the war of 1868, who became the leader of the gifted young intellectual leaders of the 1920's—Fernando Ortiz, Jorge Manach, Juan Marinello and many others—in their struggles against Machado. Such a man also was Manuel Sanguily.

A year after the Platt Amendment became law, Sanguily debated in the Senate against the Reciprocity Treaty with the United States. He said:

> The Treaty does not solve Cuba's economic problem,—at least not in Cuba's favor. On the contrary, it is one perturbation more, one new factor of confusion and derangement; cause perhaps of the widespread desperation of our lower classes who carry on their shoulders—ever with more pain— the splendor of the higher classes; and who finally, humble and ignored, decide the destiny of peoples. For the problem of reciprocity is the national problem, the basic problem of the economic and independent life of the Cubans, and it is intimately related to the problem of the American *Trusts*. First little by little, soon with alarming speed, these associations invade us, like huge octopuses enfolding us in their tentacles, to stifle our personality—every economic and general manifestation of it—to death. . . . And do not delude yourselves that these capitalist combines are a figment. They do not exist, nor could, by the mere exploitation of their business; but only through the privileges they extract from the State, subjecting it to their corruptive power.

Three weeks later, on March 28, 1903, he spoke again from the Senate floor:

Every day they leap ashore from the steamers coming from the North: these men of magnificent race, arrogant, their faces tanned by the cold north winds, with only a satchel but with wallets full of banknotes and their hearts aburst with impetuous blood; striding through our narrow streets with calculating eyes; with a supreme and changeless indifference to us. Ready to buy at low prices our immense lands. Favored by the thoughtlessness or the dire needs of the present owners who quit their patrimony without knowing what they do. And soon they will have everything. Oriente is already theirs, and the West of the island, the banks of the Cauto, the bays of Nipe and Bahia Honda. . . . And what of us? We will be powerless. . . .

Sanguily offered to the Senate a project for a law, with the following prophetic provisions:

Article I. From this date, contracts or pacts alienating land to foreigners are prohibited.

Article VI. No foreigner and no foreign corporation, of whatever class or denomination, shall build dwellings, settlements or towns without authorization of Congress beforehand and pending information as to convenience or need.

Article VII. Dwellings, settlements, etc., with the authorization referred to in the previous Article shall conform with the laws of the Republic.

Article VIII. Dwellings and settlements constructed on the grounds of old sugar *ingenios,* or any others whose population is not inferior to 250 tenants shall be incorporated into the nearest municipality, of which they will be considered districts and will be governed by the ordinances and rules of said municipality.

Article IX. Settlements larger than 250 dwellers and less than one thousand may be constituted into municipalities, if the distance to the nearest be considered too great. Those of larger number may apply to become municipalities in conformity with the laws of the Republic.

The amendments betraying and annulling Cuba's independence were in the Constitution. This bill, which at the eleventh hour sought gallantly to face Cuba's basic peril—the alienation of its land, of its law, of its wealth and of its way of life—died unread in committee.

8. *The Cubans Take Cuba*

I

WAS not the assault on the Moncada Barracks a failure? The
odds were great enough: 800 trained men and the fortress walls
against 168 youths. But the odds became hopeless when half
the cars with half the arms never reached the barracks. Over
four-fifths of the total were captured, tortured, 90 were killed.
Might one not say, a complete fiasco? Yet Castro named his
revolution for that lost day: Movimiento 26 de Julio, Cuba's
Fourth of July. This is not easy for pragmatic minds to understand. This *must* be understood, if Castro and his partners are
to be understood.

Other safer plans had been considered. They might have
taken the government radio station by surprise and called on
the people everywhere to rise against the oppressor. They might
have picked off Batista's leaders, one by one, in their homes.
They preferred a wild blow, which could be snuffed out—as it
was—with the heavily censored press stifling the news. The
news was stifled. Yet Castro counted on its getting around: news
of the assault and the failure. But could not the lesson of the
failure, when it was all known, have been the contrary of Castro's wishes; could not the lesson have been the necessity of
submission, the hopelessness of rebellion?

The Cubans are bearers of the Hispanic culture, whose hero
is Don Quixote, the knight who assails windmills and frees a
gang of brutish convicts in the desperate effort to bring justice
to the modern world. The Cubans move within what Unamuno
called "the tragic sense of life." Of course, Castro did not consciously think out the positive, symbolic meaning of his act: the
appeal of its *impossibility* to a people whose centuries had been

violence, oppression and neglect. He acted it out, with his fellows, freely offering their lives to make the *impossible* come true. Marti had already said it: "To act is agony." Castro could not know that when he was captured, Batista would not quite dare, quite *want*, to destroy him. He did know that if he was destroyed, his equals would spring up like grain from the buried seed. Castro could not know that Monsignor Enrique Perez Serantes, archbishop of Santiago, would intercede with Batista against more bloodshed, thereby saving Castro's life. He *did* know that his people understood the language of his deed: the message of Don Quixote, in whose absurdity love stands crucified and yet living; the message of the mystery that human life, under all its joys, is tragic. Much intuitive knowledge, running counter to much common sense, contributed to Castro's naming his successful revolution after that day of death.

For seventy-six days Castro remained in solitary confinement. But news of the assault, despite the silent press, began to seep through Cuba. The people were becoming vaguely aware of the young lawyer, Fidel Castro. And the dictator, uncomfortably, was aware of the people.

On October 16, Castro had his day in court. The trial was held in the hall of the school for nurses in the City Hospital of Santiago. Three judges sat. To preserve the fiction of decorum, a select small public was admitted, and six reporters. Castro conducted the defense. It took the form of a speech, later entitled *History Will Absolve Me*, which one of the reporters secretly recorded in shorthand and which, as a clandestine pamphlet of sixty pages, was soon in the hands of thousands.

Castro's argument was succinct. Flouting the law of the land, the 1940 Constitution, Batista had seized power and made himself President. Castro as a citizen of the republic, had gone before the courts and accused Batista and argued for his arraignment. The courts had refused to act. Therefore, finally, *having no other means of redress,* he and his friends had exercised *the right of insurrection* against illegal tyranny and oppression, which right lay "upon the essential base of political liberty." To prove his point, Castro the young Cuban lawyer, quoted Milton, Locke, Rousseau, Paine and finally Thomas Jefferson. "Our logic" said Castro, "is the simple logic of the people." And Castro went on, addressing the three judges, to outline—as if it were relevant to the case before them—plans for reform, primarily agrarian, which prove that already in 1953 he was working on methods for bestowing the rich land of Cuba to the Cubans.

This may have sounded, at that hour, like demagoguery to the liberals. Events were to show in it a basic principle of Castro's conduct: that no value shall be proclaimed abstractly without its immediate practical implementation.

The man already visible in the speech is indeed a man of heat (as the General Assembly of the United Nations was to find him), but of light also.

He began his fifteen-year term in the penitentiary on the Isle of Pines. The prison chief, Jesus Yanez Pelletier, received secret instructions that Castro be slowly poisoned, so that his eventual death could be ascribed to illness. Yanez did not obey, and was thrown out of the army. Meanwhile, the Moncada assault was becoming a myth among the people . . . a quiet, unassuming myth. The courage and the love within the courage, the failure and the fulfillment within failure, operated in the people as by a digestive process. As Batista's insecurity tightened and enfevered his hold on the island, the Moncada myth grew stronger. What the young heroes, ninety of them dead, had done was romantic and it appealed; their act was ethically prophetic, and this appealed more deeply.

Batista in 1953 still had hopes of winning the favor of the people; therefore, he had listened to the archbishop pleading no more bloodshed; and therefore now, in March 1954, he proclaimed an amnesty which opened the prison doors for Castro and his surviving friends. Declaring that he and his colleagues abjured none of their convictions, Castro returned to Havana, and soon learned he could do nothing there within the cruel iron ring of Batista's soldiers. He went to New York, and found it too remote; finally to Mexico, where he began to study plans for the delivery of Cuba to the Cubans.

II

What was the state of Cuba? All, and worse, had come that Manuel Sanguily feared would come, a half-century before. Fewer than twelve hundred individuals and individual corporations owned most of the sugar and industrial plants and the mines. The vast majority of these owners were foreign, and the majority of these foreigners were Americans. Mining concessions had been so lavishly, so immorally extended that they summed to a total acreage greater than the real total area of the country! The alienation of the Cuban agricultural worker from his soil was almost complete. The chief occupation was sugar, which calls for only four months' labor in the year. Since Big Business and alien ownership were not interested in the Cubans' problem of what to eat, nonemployment of hundreds of thousands over large portions of the year was endemic. The Cuban peasant was no peasant; he was a part-time industrial slave attached to a factory whose product went to the world and whose profits went, by overwhelming preponderance, to the United States. Some of this outflow of wealth returned, not to Cuba but to Havana in forms eloquently proclaimed by the luxury hotels, the night clubs and casinos. A whole class throve in Havana on this wealth: prostitutes and prostituted artists, gamblers, procurers and always politicians. None more important than these political pimps—taking their cut—who attended to the details of parceling out Cuba to the aliens.

The process, of course, was not unique to Cuba; most Latin American countries shared the economic colonialism but in mitigated forms. None of the nations, except Panama, had been born attached to the United States by such a bond as the Platt Amendment, so that the statesmen elsewhere did not need to stultify their actions with the false premise of independence. Cuba was the archetype, with its maximum closeness to the United States, forever driving down into the Caribbean; with its maximum wealth and its long-suffering *guajiro*, wracked by maladies of malnutrition, naked and exiled from his Eden.

Here is the Cuba which explains Castro, now in Mexico with two hundred of his friends, all being drilled in the arts of war by a veteran of Spain's war against Franco, Colonel Alberto Bayo, all studying the economics of their beloved problem, how to turn over Cuba to the Cubans.

Batista was the most interesting of the corrupt Presidents of Cuba, but he was not the first, not the most successful. Before him came Gerardo Machado, who dominated the arena and the spoils (1925–1933) before Batista's first rise to power by an army *Putsch* in 1936.

Machado was the plain businessman in the Cuban business of politics, which consisted of maneuvering for places where he could get his fingers, and finally both hands, into the public till. His eminence was entirely due to perseverance and thoroughness in offering and delivering favors. Never much liked, nor caring, he bought himself (chiefly with promises of graft) the Liberal party nomination for President. Mussolini was his ideal —but he dispensed with the demagoguery and the *mystique*. He "improved" Cuba (mostly Havana), and each contract meant a spreading of the spoils.

Machado built the Carretera Central, the first hard-surfaced road along the entire spine of Cuba. He built the Malecon, the brilliant highway that girds Havana to the sea. He built the Capitolio, that lavish imitation of the Washington, D.C., original, an architectural monster which rhetorically announces to the world Cuba's past servitude to the United States. (When peace frees the resources of Cuba, this aggressive reminder of the false republic must be razed.) Once in power, Machado ceased to be the negotiator, the manipulator, and became the tyrant, convinced that his first duty was to remain in office. He developed a secret police whose task was to eliminate dissenters. Rival politicians, labor leaders, intellectuals with awkward ideas about the workers, were shot as they came out of their homes or stepped into a car. Students were persecuted; several were murdered. Finally, the university classes were suspended. Batista is supposed to have killed 20,000 in his years of maintaining order in which business could flourish. Machado could not equal this; he specialized in the elimination of potential leaders. He would not, like Batista, have spared the life of Castro because of a sentimental need to curry favor with the people.

In 1929, President Herbert Hoover sent Harry F. Guggenheim as U.S. Ambassador to Havana. Guggenheim was a very rich young man of very meager mind. He had other credentials. Son of Daniel, eldest brother of the great copper family, he was of course close to Anaconda (Cuba is rich in copper and nickel), and involved with such interests as the National City Bank (which controlled much of Cuba's sugar), Bethlehem Steel (which had staked out claims on Cuba's immense and virgin iron deposits) and Remington Arms (which supplied Machado's army). He was close to other Cuban powers, such as Electric Bond and Share, International T&T, and the Cuban-American Manganese Corporation, which possessed 10,000 acres of Cuba's mineral land. As a business deal, the appointment was appropriate; and what was Cuba but "business" to the corporations which owned it and to Machado who ran it for them?

A great friendship grew between the ambassador and Machado. They worked together and they played together. The ambassador relaxed at Machado's palatial yacht club; the President gave the ambassador a black Arab steed for his morning constitutional rides. Machado was already declining into the grim last phase of his rule, before revolution overthrew him, when murder was his method. This did not trouble the young man who knew the perfume of money better than the smell of blood that money covered. So close were the two that Guggenheim was constantly intervening in the presidential office. It became common knowledge that the American, "*the*" Embassy, was the door to Cuban action. Guggenheim went farther. He encouraged Machado's friends and he discouraged Machado's enemies. As Machado's resolve to hold on grew more desperate, Guggenheim's resolve to help him came ever closer to intervention.[1]

Fulgencio Batista is a more complicated figure. His face reveals mestizo origins common in the bays and mountains of Oriente, which through the centuries have been exposed to infiltrations of Indians from Yucatan and of Negroes from Haiti and Santo Domingo. But Batista's cloudiness is psychological. Of humblest birth, he began to irradiate his extraordinary influence in the army, when he was a mere stenographer-sergeant. His quick mind absorbed everything he wrote down, and its extrapolations. He learned a cynical version of his country, but he wanted to be loved by his people. He tried to build schools and dwellings, but his graft obligations set their cost too high. It was cheaper to buy uniforms for an army of gunmen.

In 1936 the army gave him power. In 1940 he "won" the election, thanks to wholesale fraud at the polls. In 1952, learning that he was a poor third among the candidates, he crashed into office again with the army and abolished the coming elections. (This was the occasion described by Castro in his defense speech.) The hunger to be loved did not fade. The thwarted lover becomes the sadist; when the embrace is not accepted, it may be replaced by the cruel hand. And as the people shrank, the sadist became more cruel. Moreover, the sadist in power draws sadists to him. Under a rule such as Batista's, the psychotically cruel (who exist in every land) become soldiers and policemen, and through the satisfaction of their sickly need enact the frustrated need of the dictator. But the sadist, the thwarted lover, returns time and again to wooing his beloved. In his amnesty, Batista wooed the people.

Machado . . . Guggenheim . . . Batista . . . must be recognized

1. The reader who wants the full details of the unsavory story is referred to Carleton Beals' excellent book, *The Crime of Cuba* (Philadelphia: Lippincott, 1933).

as immediately present in Mexico where Castro and his men are learning the arts of guerilla warfare. And the Cuban people are present. The *guajiro* is a paradoxical figure. Miserable, he is capable of tremendous effort. Passive and submissive, like a carnivorous beast he can burst into action yet keep his head like a man. His centuries have been tragic, yet he has wit, a bright tongue, high spirits, because he has the wisdom to know that the tragedy and the joy of living must be together.

There is another presence in Mexico, as the *ignition* of Cuba is prepared: the United States. The Cubans admire the American civilization and distrust what they call its culture. They do not know America by statistics, but even the illiterate have an intuitive sense of the world around them. Vaguely, organically, they feel the pressure and the gravity of a nation that spends in a year $38 billion for new cars, billions for cosmetics, a quarter-billion for tranquillizers, and a mere $2.5 billion for new schools. This, to them, is a nervous, restless and drugged people, in an intellectual, emotional and spiritual coma induced—if not by drugs—by television. Dimly the Cubans realize that the United States of Jefferson and Lincoln is also a *betrayed* republic.

Castro was once asked his opinion of Batista. It was a meditative moment (there are few such moments in Castro's night and day), when the questioner and he were flying over the vast swamp of the peninsula of Zapata. Castro drew on his long cigar and pondered long before he answered: "He is a stupid man. He showed it, when he refused to take us seriously in the Sierra Maestra. He showed it. . . ." Castro's voice stopped, but the questioner felt that he was thinking of the time when the dictator could have killed him. In the word "stupid," he was implying a complexity of judgments: that he (Castro) could have been eliminated and the revolution would yet have continued; that Batista was evil and it is the nature of evil men to be stupid; and that the simple "stupidity" of all Cuba's foes could be relied upon. Revealed in the unfinished sentence was both the strength of Castro's indubitable goodness and its potential weakness. For the reality was more complex, Batista was more complex than Castro figured. But if Castro consciously reckoned on all the complexities, he would often be stayed, or at least slowed, in his actions, which have in them an integral sense of Cuba and of Cuba's need. Also revealed in the unfinished sentence was an unreally simple view of the complexities of Cuba's world position.

Castro's equally off-the-record words to the same questioner, a year after the Zapata flight, in his hotel room in Harlem, show a change. We had been speaking of Israel, and Castro had to leave for a second meeting with Nasser the Egyptian. Back and forth in the narrow bedroom, Castro paced, wringing his hands and saying over and over: "It's complex! It's so complex. How complex everything is!" To this questioner it was plain that Castro was capable of growing.

III

They were having plenty of trouble in Mexico. The police found them and threatened to confiscate their dearly bought arms. Castro spent months in prison. At last, the final November week of 1956, all is ready. A half open launch, sixty-two feet in length, its rotted timbers freshly painted white and green, holds the arms and the eighty-two men. Castro has announced by radio that he is coming. Some of his advisers, including Colonel Bayo, remind him of the Spanish saying, "*Guerra avisada no mata soldado*," "A battle announced kills no soldier." Fidel is faithful to his vision; he and his men are a mere fuse and may go the way of fuses: the fire will be Cuba, and the people of Cuba must know that they are coming.

The leaky boat, a Greek vessel called *Gramma*, bought at a low price that is high considering its dubious seaworthiness, crawls from the little harbor of Tuxpan. Five days combating wind and wave convey it to the extreme south coast of Oriente. Rough seas disrupt the landing. Before the eighty-two men with their assembled arms, rise the highest of Cuba's mountains, the

Sierra Maestra, Castro's choice for the birthplace of Cuban Cuba.

One of the men on that journey was asked how they spent the five days. "*Vomitando,* " was the answer. "We vomited." It is Dr. Ernesto Guevara speaking. "At first we made the effort to rid ourselves over the gunwales; to keep some semblance of cleanliness aboard. Soon we did not care. We vomited where we sat or lay: on the floor, on the benches, on our clothes and on each other." In this anguish of a little overloaded craft, tossed, rolled and twisted by the seas, the purpose of the journey never receded, and there were no regrets. Finally the time—the Cuban time—for laughing at themselves began.

The eighty-two landed, and at once split into small groups, for Batista had been alerted by Castro himself and there were planes (American-made) already in the air above them. Some of the men died on the beach where a mountain stream, carrying Cuba to them, joined it. Others got safely lost, groping their way westward. Many were caught, tortured and killed. Only a few, who made for the near mountains, got safely through the thorny jungle, the *managua,* that interceded. Fidel and his little group of eleven men aimed at the highest peak, the Turquino. They lived on berries (a physician among them knew the good from the bad); they sucked arum root whose meat is sinewy and coarse; or they got contributions—rare at first—from the suspicious mountain peasants. Castro paid for every offering.

The Sierra Maestra is a lush wilderness. The red earth seems deep and distant under the green, rugose mountain folds. Growth of tree and fern is thick, never admitting the sun, framing a dark, damp cosmos. Ferns in this swampy air are higher than a man, but pines flourish also, and palms. The mountains are fugues of verdure, but they are also articulations of a telluric body, like limbs, like shoulders. And there are clearings, in which the sun falls without hindrance.

This was the site of Castro's new republic.

Batista's planes kept sweeping low over the jungle in search of Castro and his men, dropping bombs blindly. To cheat the spies and scouts, Castro and his fellows never slept two nights in the same spot. The Havana papers pronounced his invasion scattered like ashes, and himself dead. But he was judged to have many lives; for although he was dead, the planes kept on looking for him.

The *campesinos* found him and began to join him. (They were welcome only if they brought a gun, or at least a long machete.) The young men of the towns also found him: youths from Bayamo, Camaguey, Santa Clara and Havana. Women also made their way to his shifting quarters: among them Celia Sanchez, whom the reader has already met in Harlem and in the Assembly of the United Nations.

The Sierra republic, whose aim was to release the captured and prostrate republic of Batista, lived and grew because it was dynamic. It was not a promise or a "date" in the future; not a refuge, not a haven; it was a *focus*, electric, endowed with the principle of growth, both additive and selective, like the cells in a young body. When Castro first arrived, he needed to make contact with the mountain peasants in order not to starve. If this need of his belly had been all, or the main motive, the *guajiro* would have known it as a dog knows the motive of a man's approach. But there had been for years, in Castro, love for the miserable Cuban peasant. Now he, Castro, was more miserable than the man before him. The *guajiro* knew this and gave the corn; soon he gave himself, coming up to the summit of El Plata, perhaps bearing with him an old rifle. There was no fraudulence in this alliance. (And it has lasted.)

In the constantly changing camps there began to appear both freedom and routine. Men (and women, too) were *going to school* in the Sierra Maestra.

The wilderness of Sinai was *a school* for the children of Israel; it was a sterile wilderness but for the *mana* of the Lord. Here, the mana was sugar and *malanga,* within a plethora of fertile nature. Here in the Sierra from the very start, the agrarian reform was thrashed out and hammered into shape by argument and application; the urban reform, too, which was not to become law until the end of 1960.

The first attack on a Batista garrison village was the raid of La Plata at the foot of the range of Turquino, Cuba's highest peak. This took place one month and fifteen days after the landing of the *Gramma* at Belic. Here Castro had set up his first sedentary quarters, a shack with a tin roof. The first Bedouin phase of his campaign was over. The raids, whose chief aim was arms, meant encounter almost always with detachments of Batista's army, ten times as numerous as the rebels. The professionals of Batista wanted to live, had nothing to risk their lives for, and were afraid. The young *rebeldes* wanted to live also, but only on their terms, a free Cuba for which they were ready to run risks. Moreover, there were good minds in Castro's camp. Batista's mercenaries, although trained by American officers, had no teachers to match men of advanced and disciplined intelligence such as Ernesto Guevara, Camillo Cienfuegos, Juan Almeida, Antonio Nuñez Jimenez and Raul Castro.

The tiny free republic spread. The advance from the start was an organic movement, and complex: even the leaders were not conscious of it all, for much of it took place in the reticent minds of peasants—peasants convinced that Fidel Castro knew what he said, and meant what he did. Batista's soldiers began to cross the lines and join the *rebelde* camps. More important: peasants and the folk of humble villages tasted the process going on before them, and liked it. Castro immediately turned over recovered lands to the men who had always worked them. Small factories were established: one of the first was for shoes, and soon there was a gun-repair shop with an electric lathe and a tin shop that made grenades out of old cans. And every set-up was a classroom fended by ferns and pines from the forever roving enemy planes. Wherever he was, Castro talked, making the place a classroom.

These talks were not doctrinal, beyond the doctrine of Marti that Cuba belonged to the Cubans, that Cuba must be an active organ of America Hispana's Bolivarian will to create a new world of social justice in the hemisphere. Marxism, strictly interpreted by arguing theorists, the heirs of arguing theolgians, determined the temper and pressure of the young revolutionists of Russia, produced the dogmatisms and puritanisms of the Communist revolutionists of Russia, and produced the dogmatisms and puritanisms of Communist revolutions everywhere. The youth of Cuba, mobilized by Castro, were far more flexible. The lush, overrich land of Cuba released them before they could be stereotyped by dogma. What they made was autochthonous, and needed no name beyond the life, the joyous life, they spontaneously shared.

Connections grew with the cities: from Santiago to Pinar del Rio, the whole length of the island. They began "underground." Frank Pais, until his death in 1958, conducted a system in Santiago; Faustino Perez, a former physician, who had given up his practice to help the Cubans conquer Cuba, laid subterranean lines from the Sierra Maestra clear to Havana. Soon the little republic was a going concern. It had bakeshops and a weekly paper, and before long a *Radio Rebelde* to refute the servile press of Batista, which kept on reporting Castro dead.

In May 1958, Batista launched his offensive. The *rebeldes* were so widely outnumbered that in places a dozen men or boys faced a battalion. Inch by inch, they yielded ground, drawing the enemy into the mountains, into the exact positions decided on beforehand by the strategists under the tin roof of El Plata. They knew the terrain, every foot. And Batista's offensive dragged on, finally bogged down. The prisoners caught by the regulars were shot.

After four months, Batista's army was where the *rebeldes* wanted it to be and the counteroffensive began. Soon hundreds of the regulars were captured. If wounded, they were treated in the improvised field hospitals. All were sent home—unless they decided to fight along with their former foes. Castro explained on the air: "If they remained with us as prisoners our scarce supplies of food, medicines and cigarettes would have to be shared. Moreover, they are Cubans. We must live with them, and they must live with us, in every village. Why not begin at once?" Of course, the soldiers who went home told of their humane treatment.

None of the Cuban political parties in the first year supported Castro. The Communists frowned on "the romantic bourgeois nationalist revolution, " smiled at its lack of theory. The bearded boys in the Sierra Maestra were, for the strict Marxists, anachronisms. Their roots were in Marti and in Heredia (both poets); above all in the bourgeois Spanish tradition of the *Comuneros*. Not until power rolled Castro and his little nation down Machado's Carretera Central to Havana did the Communists approve. Then, impressed, they jumped on the bandwagon.

What of the liberals?

The *rebeldes* came down from the Sierra to the valley. Raul Castro set up a "second front" in northeastern Oriente; Juan Almeida, a "third front" between Santiago and El Cobre. Ernesto Guevara, the former psychiatrist of Buenos Aires, and Camillo Cienfuegos, a man beautiful as a god, led columns of specially schooled fighters north and south respectively to the central province of Las Villas and cut the island in two. It was becoming clear even to the liberals (many in exile) that Castro's army, reinforced with men and material from Batista's army, was going to win. They formed what they called "The Council of Liberation." Participating in it were the Partido Revolucionario Cubano, the Partido del Pueblo Cubano, the Organizacion Autentica, the Federacion Estudiantil Universitaria, the Directorio Revolucionario and the Directorio Obrero Revolucionario. Cuba's active and best-known democrats led them, for the most part from exile. They sent Castro a cordial letter inviting him to pool his forces and his leadership with theirs.

Since before Machado, these liberals had endeavored, in and out of office, to calm and to cure Cuba without disturbing the causes of its fever. They wanted to reform, not transfigure. They were good men, or perhaps men of good words: Justice, Democracy. But Castro was of a tribe of prophets who took words to heart at heart value, and made them into deed. He knew how the gradualism of these men was like a sluggish stream that dies in a desert. With his intuition he appeared to know that in the heart of most liberals there is the fear of a new world that cannot be gauged or trained (by them) beforehand—a new world that is a birth, therefore unaccountable and unruly. Castro did not disdain the liberals' offer; he evaded the impedimenta and the drag of their good will. He answered their letter courteously, declining their offer.

Then he sent a note to the President of the United States. "Sir," he said in effect, "there is a state of war in Cuba. You should be neutral; yet you support one side. At least stop sending them arms and military missions." The State Department answered for the President. Regimes, it said in effect, come and go in Cuba. But the defense of the hemisphere against an insidious alien foe: *that* is important, and *that* is why the United States will keep on sending arms and missions to the recognized government of Cuba.

Only in December did the mission and the ammunition cease: two weeks before Batista, on January 1, 1959, fled the country with loot estimated at 400 million dollars.[2]

IV

All the way from Oriente to Pinar del Rio, young men— young women, too—moved into abandoned municipal posts and sent their love to the Sierra Maestra, asking for instructions. Officials who had been loyal to Batista fled or surrendered. The commander of the Moncada Barracks, which had "destroyed" the *rebeldes* five years before, announced to Raul Castro, who was nearby, that the fortress gates were open to receive him.

2. This is the estimate of the revolutionary government. But I know of no reliable figures for the graft and the loot. Faustino Perez, former Minister "de Recuperacion de Bienes Nacionales"—a ministry that has since been abolished as a separate department, informed me that in the first year 35 million were recovered, and that it was known that Batista had 3.5 million stashed away in safe-deposit bank boxes in New York.

The protocol of the conventional Hispano-American revolution now required that the new leader make a triumphal march as soon as possible to the Presidential Palace. By all precedent, Fidel Castro behaved strangely. He did not fly to Havana. He did not start for Havana. He paid a visit to his old mother on the family hacienda in Oriente (she had not seen him since his escape to Mexico.) He considered making Santiago the capital of his republic. And when he was asked about Havana, his extraordinarily mobile face, more feminine in its sensitivity than one might expect of so massive and burly a warrior, expressed distaste, reluctance, even pique. He sent out a message:

> Each of us, we are soldiers of the Fatherland. We do not belong to ourselves. We belong to our country. No matter that some of us fall. What matters is that the flag waves on high; that the Revolution goes forward and that the Fatherland lives.

This is a position one may dissent from. One may recognize in it the perils of collective egoism and of over-simplification, two dangerous world trends of our time. One may ask, where is there room in such an absolute nationalist position, for the *person* with the cosmos in him? The *person* whose value and health may be beyond the collective ego of the nation? The point here is that it was Castro's position, as he saw and meant it. From its premise, a Roman triumph into the capital city was wrong and Castro did not like it, and it therefore did not figure in Castro's program.

Havana, with all its flags unfurled, began to murmur.

Then something unexampled happened.

The agrarian workers of Cuba, cutters and grinders of the cane, dwellers on Cuba's land, which was not theirs, dwellers in hovels and huts not fit to be pigsties, began to converge from north and south upon the central Carretera, and to move toward Havana. No one in authority had told them to come or how to come or what to do when they arrived. By the hundreds, by the thousands, they were coming, they were closing in. They came by truck, standing, close-packed. They came by requisitioned buses. They came in carts smelling of manure, drawn by mule. Most of them came by foot. And as they marched the hot and hungry miles upon Havana (which most of them had never seen) a voice rose from them—FIDEL—and became a marching song: FIDEL! FIDEL!

Castro heard it. This was no Roman military triumph. This was *orders* from the people. A helicopter stood in the backyard of the farm where he had lived as a boy, and Castro boarded it. It hovered low over the wide valley of the Carretera, over the thousands of heads which went up to greet it and as if to hold it in the air. FIDEL! Castro was thus figuratively *carried* to Havana by the people.

When they got there, the many hundred thousands, another spontaneous event cleared the threatened stifling of the city. Havana has innumerable rooms: rooms of rooming houses of the poor, rooms of humble people, luxurious rooms of the rich, hotel rooms, rooms of prostitutes and pimps and gamblers. Havana threw open all its rooms to the sea of invaders. They were fed in the kitchens, they were bunked on the floors. Food stores were flung open without price. The Havana houses, wide open, became mouths to sing a song of thanks. For the first time in its four centuries of dolor, Cuba felt itself free. The young folks and the old, milling through the central modern avenues, the blooming plazas, the ancient narrow streets, gave forth song. The buildings, dirty and crumbling or chromium and pastel bright, gave forth song.

Spontaneous acts of a people are far rarer than the sun. But like the sun, obedient to a law, they know when to rise and when to wane. Thus, the jubilant waves receded. The rooms, a good deal dirtier, shut their doors and their windows. Cuba goes back to Cuba—leaving Castro and his group of helmsmen to obey this mandate of the people, to grapple with the problems of creating a nation.

9. Methods and Men

THE business of Cuba in the hands of Cuba's people was a heavy, intricate load: economically, psychologically and politically a complex load. The war of the *rebeldes* had not razed the country as did the wars of Gomez, Maceo and Garcia, since it was a struggle primarily of moral attrition. But the cynical corruption of resources had gutted the land as a producing instrument. Cuba was a factory of sugar, but this did not make it efficient; its use of its wealth and its manpower was pitifully limited. Waste was the rule, and neglect. Even food was imported to the rich, underpopulated island.

Symbolic of the state of Cuba were the fields overgrown with the thorny and impassable *marabu* under which the loam remained virgin. This explains why, despite the dislocations of the agrarian reform and the inexperience and errors of the new order, Cuba immediately became more productive: the statistics are there to prove it. Unemployment, which had been endemic and to which the ruling alien powers were indifferent, declined and in some parts of the island vanished. So much needed to be done that much was done spontaneously, through the simple fact that a whole body of labor had been released into action. Roads spanned unworked lands and swamps; fields were cleared and the rank shrubs turned to charcoal. Hundreds of cooperatives, agricultural and commercial, distributed the fruits of work to the workers. Rice, cotton, henequen, corn, challenged the sugar monoculture. Tens of thousands of new classrooms required teachers from every village, who were turned out by "crash" capsule courses. Under Batista illiteracy had increased; but 1961 was proclaimed by Armando Hart, the Minister of

Education, as the year for its total extinction. Barracks became schools. Schools became foci of adult education.

Economic advances had the impact of the explosions in a cylinder. But they were not alone. Centers of sport, of play (stressed by Castro) and of cultivation of the arts and letters shared in the released and rising power of the nation. Nationalized factories, refineries and markets called for technicians, and almost overnight men who had no technical training were compelled by the momentum of events to go to school, even while running the businesses which previously employed them. Literally, the face of Cuba changed. The reconstruction went deep and wide. The *rebelde* army became a task force largely organized under the INRA. One can justly say that the army disbanded the army, and in its place rose the armed youth and the armed girls. Each evening, in every village and town, one heard their footsteps as they drilled. *Patria o Muerte.*

Like all youth they are not concerned with death, which was far too distant for their eager eyes. But their *Patria* existed! Prepared to die to defend it against its enemies at home and abroad, they could touch their fatherland, and explore it. When Castro showed a visitor a new development of low-rent houses east of Havana, his hands outstretched to cover its scope and its approach to the sea where playgrounds and bathing beaches for the humble were planned, one could feel his sense of possession, as if the island lay really within his arms: the whole island! And precisely the same sentiment of possession was in the boys and girls drilling . . . *uno* . . . *dos* . . . *tres* . . . *cuatro* . . . in the evening-cool plazas. The revolution was their way of life, which meant, since they are young, that it had its romanticism and its sentimentalism.

To one who has breakfasted, breakfast is a prosaic fact of the past, without emotional load. To one who has not broken fast, it is an urgent, glamorous hope. So many Americans are worried about overeating, not about getting breakfast! So many have forgotten Valley Forge! Likewise, a well-regulated household takes its plumbing for granted. How can it understand the *hallelujah* of the Cubans when the tap is turned and the clear water flows?

There is another cause for romanticism in any revolution: the close presence of its enemies. In the American Revolution, 80,000 of the 3.5 million inhabitants left their homes and fled to Canada and England. Other thousands with Tory sentiments sullenly remained. They sharpened the self-righteousness of the republicans, for whom they became "villains." A revolution always profits (if it wins) by martyrdom and the threat of external oppression. The revolution becomes "perfect"; the nationalization, as in the case of Cuba, becomes an end in itself—like the brand-new breakfast. This is what we designate as "romantic." Some of the bellicosity of Castro toward the State Department doubtless is of this nature, although the Cuban people have cause enough, in hard fact, to feel threatened.

The romantic element in Cuba's revolution is therefore understandable, but can cause trouble because it is not accurate. A nation can be as faulty as a human being; a nation unjustly attacked does not thereby become a paragon. Many young Cubans do not quite know this. For example, they do not know that the mere nationalization of their industries—a necessity as a means of striking clear of the *Yanquis*—is no goal, that it may enthrone a bureaucracy even more rigid than capitalist possession. Castro's summary act of nationalization was an intelligent, courageous deed, required to enlist the people and to remove huge, hostile economic and political forces from a position within the republic from which they could and would destroy it. But nationalization is not necessarily true socialization, an end which demands that there be workers in each industry competent to run it and to coordinate with all the others. These are needs, aims, hazards, which the romantic does not envisage; whence may come puzzlement, disillusion, corruption, inefficiency and despair—unto the aggressiveness of counterrevolution. Witness the withdrawal from reality of the present "beat" generation in Western nations—which had its equivalent in the reactions from the bourgeois romantic revolutions of the eighteenth and nineteeth centuries. Touching the crises that are sure to come in Cuba (as in other phases of the world revolution), we come to the problems of leadership and of leaders.

For example: by the law of Urban Reform, promulgated in October 1960, the landlord who collects over $600 monthly in rents loses that excess to the nation; and a family which has been paying rent over the years finds that what it has paid is to be counted toward ownership of its dwelling. Since the value of real estate depends on growth of, and use by, the population, what could be more just? But cool heads in the government of Cuba—Guevara, for one—already know that "this is not so simple." There will be trying complications. People will want to move to other towns and provinces. People will want to sell and to buy.

Another example of the complexity of reform: one of the first visitors to Cuba Libre was Lazaro Cardenas, the former President of Mexico. He came to explain to Castro and his leaders why the Mexico *ejido* system of communal farms failed. There was not sufficient economic aid to validate possession through increased production; and there was not sufficient defense against the banks, against creditors taking the land, and against debtors losing it. Cuban directors went to school under the great Mexican. Cuba is full of technical economic problems, and technicians are not formed overnight. Already in the Sierra Maestra, Castro knew the need for proper *methods,* if the people's basic will—riddance of the tyrant and of the conditions that breed tyrants—was to be effective. The people must have method and means, to hold in their hands what their hands created.

Technicians are indeed not born, but they can be imported. They have come, from the Soviet Union, Czechoslovakia, Canada, Poland, China, Japan, to replace American technicians whose economic-cultural principles were alien and unwelcome. But how is Cuba to be sure that the newcomers, needed to run the nationalized industries and to set up the new factories, will not have brought, suffused in their techniques, another ideology, equally alien, equally unwelcome? For an ideology may be implicit in the most objective methods for manufacturing the most objective products. From an American car, for instance—that "arrogant chariot," as Lewis Mumford called it—much can be spelled out about American values and the reigning American ethos.

As I revise this chapter, I read of an agreement between Cuba and the Soviet Union by which a thousand Soviet youths are to come to Cuba each year to learn Cuban agricultural methods in exchange for one thousand young Cubans who will go to Russia to learn Soviet methods. Who doubts that the Cuban youth will be affected by the values of the Soviets, both dogmatic and implicit? The answer to such a cultural problem is, of course, more exchange of more students with more countries, not retreat behind a collective-ego curtain and not the manufacture of more bombs and more rhetoric about hemisphere independence. The creative answer is to be relaxed, inviting and aware. This is work for leaders.

The leaders in Cuba today, at least those I have known, are aware of such problems and sure they can cope with them. They will tell you in plain words that they have not overthrown the overlordship of the United States in order to submit to a new master.[1] Perhaps they are romantic, too, like the confident boys and girls who drill in the streets. It is, however, a surprising fact that for fifty years Cuba has been invaded unto saturation by the cultural values of the United States, and has come up with adverse judgment—unto repudiation. The Cubans have not liked what they got from the United States, nor what they saw: not succumbed, and also not fearfully rejected. *They have chosen.* And they are convinced that they can still choose; are convinced that the powers of a technological civilization,

1. A little incident reveals much. Waldo Medina, who occupies a government post analogous to that of our Attorney-General, sent a new trade contract with the Russians to Ernesto Guevara, who leads the National Bank. The contract had a clause to the effect that any controversy or disagreement arising should be referred to a court of arbitration in Moscow. Guevara crossed out this clause and wrote in the margin of the contract: "We have not got free of one master to take on another."

producing the possibility of plenty for all, can be *geared into* a humanism (Castro's word) which translates yet does not lose the *personal* values of the Hispanic-Judaeo-Christian culture. The men around Castro, who speak his language and who accept him because he has proved himself able to convey their meanings into deeds, are either articulate enough to say this or implicitly affirm it. They are technicians, methodologists of government; how good, how strong in their tasks, the future will tell. This to me is sure: they are *good men* and what they are attempting in their imperiled world is *good*.

I can hear the protests: *How do you know? What is a good man?* Men in power—political, industrial, ecclesiastical—usually impress one with their love of power, their love of the game of power, their love of the status which entrenches their ego, their skills of diplomacy, their glibness and charm, by anything but their goodness. Why not these men of Cuba?

Thomas Hardy, deepest of British novelists, wrote in one of his diaries:

> It is the incompleteness that is loved, when love is sterling and true. This is what differentiates the real one from the imaginary, the practical from the impossible, the Love who returns the kiss from the Vision that melts away. A man sees the Diana or the Venus in his Beloved, but what he loves is the difference.

This is a key to what I mean by goodness. These men have their share of weaknesses and lusts. But preponderantly and devotedly they are in love with Cuba's incompleteness, and with the task (they have all risked life for it) of Cuba's self-fulfillment as a people. Alas! Since they are men and women, there is nothing necessarily permanent in this goodness. If the day comes when they love Cuba possessively for what it gives *them*, for what they have given *it, and for what it is now,* they will cease to be good leaders.

We have already met some of these leaders: Antonio Nuñez

Jimenez, the happy man who runs INRA and whose playful energies explore caves and fossils as if they were light beamed into the dark of geological earth; Raul Roa, the intensely modern intellectual whose lineage links him with America Hispana's great liberal tradition (his grandfather, the friend of Marti, was for years the secretary of Sarmiento, Argentina's great schoolmaster President); and Celia Sanchez, the "housekeeper" of the establishment. The romantic element of the movement was perhaps best expressed by Camillo Cienfuegos, the blond, tall Adonis with the flamboyant golden beard and lusty blue eyes of a Viking, whose dauntless courage made him the revolution's outstanding captain. Cienfuegos boarded a small Cessna plane in Camaguey, bound for Havana, and was lost with the pilot in a storm that blew them out to sea. His death was, in a sense, a symbol of the beginning of the end of the romantic phase of Cuba's revolution.[2]

Very different is Armando Hart Davalos, the twenty-eight-year-old Minister of Education. At first glance, Hart's good looks and neat eloquence might cause doubts: is he of "Madison Avenue," as it may be, when the founders of Wall Street and Philistia find another home there? Under the lubricated surface, Hart is a dedicated man, no less intensely than Roa or Nuñez Jimenez. His wife is the key to his drive. Haydee Santa Maria was one of the two women who went the tragic and prophetic way to the Moncada Barracks. With her brother, she was captured and tortured. His gouged eye was brought to her on a plate to make her talk. She did not talk, and her brother died. Hart's glance at her, when they are now in company to-

---

2. The instances of false and falsely slanted reporting about Cuba in the American press are innumerable. Often the misleading has been confined to the headlines, which the text contradicts. How it handled this story is typical. It did not accuse, it merely mentioned the rumor that Cienfuegos had escaped to the United States, or that he had been done away with by Castro, or that the plane was sabotaged. There is no evidence of this. The government declared a week of public mourning for the lost hero, a fact which was not recorded in many newspapers to balance the rumors.

gether and her face suddenly breaks with pain, makes clear where he belongs: he is the ruthless servant of the revolution. Hart has read both John Dewey and Marx—and their fertile dissenters, such as Harold Rugg. Much of his work is conventional: his public lectures, his dance and music recitals open to the people for a nominal sum. But the teachers he is producing for his tens of thousands of new classrooms reveal the man's quality of leadership: for they are tender, sensitive daughters and daring sons of the Cuban earth.

None of the men around Castro has received more comment than Ernesto Guevara, *"el Ché,"* the Argentinian who is often referred to as the icy Marxist "eminence" behind the throne. Guevara was a psychiatrist, practicing psychoanalysis in Buenos Aires. He came to the conclusion that Freudian therapy errs basically in its acceptance of the present social order as a norm. His thoughts about social revolution coincided, he found, with much in Marx; only in this convergence, he says, might he be called a Marxist. But he is not an organization man, not a Communist. In his early phases he might be called "an adventurer." He became one of Castro's extraordinary captains, applying his intellect to the tasks of war. But his connection with Cuba, which may have begun as an adventurous "love affair," has long since become a marriage. Guevara's intelligence is of the basic, conceptual kind that may be modulated toward many objects and forms. The therapist becomes the revolutionist . . . becomes the soldier . . . becomes the administrator of Cuba's industry . . . becomes the banker . . . becomes the arbiter of Cuba's trade agreements with other countries. Guevara's appearance can mislead. His round face with blonde disheveled hair and straggly beard seems cherubic—until one meets his eyes, which are hard-black and firm. In his mussed fatigue uniform of a *Rebelde,* he seems casual and careless, but his record reveals not only an immense capacity for work but also a considerable power of organization. His mind and its training give him detachment. I recall one night when for hours he expounded to me, with all the mental batteries of the therapist, how a man feels who kills an enemy—all in a soft voice, ingratiating as a whisper.

There are certain analogies, as well as deep differences, between Guevara and Fidel Castro's brother, Raul. He also is supposed, without evidence, to be a Communist. Raul is a tough and clever fighter, now at the head of the Ministry of Defense. Tall, youthful, until recently he tried to grow a beard (it came out like spots of henequen or cactus in a desert). Before going abroad on a visit, he shaved the poor beard off. There is nothing unvirile about Raul (his marriage with Vilma Espin is a good one); yet he is affectionate, modest, capable of silence and of sensitive responses. His famed ruthlessness in war I must accept on report. When he was asked if he was a Communist, he replied: "If I were a Communist I would say so." Raul is not a university man like his brother; the revolution swept him out of school. Ideology, I suspect, means little to him and could not be the cause of his *not* accepting communism. I think the reason is probably that he finds all he needs by way of doctrine in the nationalism and the Hispano-Americanism of Marti.

The President of Cuba, Oswaldo Dorticos, differs from most of his colleagues in having passed the ripe old age of forty. He was a highly successful lawyer in Cienfuegos, an urban, cultured liberal of the upper class, whose observance of the fate of gradualism in Mexico, Chile, Peru and Western Europe led to his vigorous support of Castro. Dorticos is no figurehead, as many want to believe. His influence is wide because his versatility is subtle. He is not a gradualist in doctrine (the shapes of the new laws come largely from him), yet can be a gradualist in his tactics of personal relations—both with the people who love his speeches and with his colleagues.

The outstanding, the frightening trait of Fidel Castro is, of course, his rejection of gradualism. In this sense, and this alone, he is the great disciple of the nineteeth-century Venezuelan socialist, Daniel De Leon, the one man, according to Lenin, to add a creative contribution to the theories of Marx. De Leon was opposed to that collaboration between workers and capitalist society, which has been the rule of the Western welfare republics. In a brilliant study of the imperialism of Rome, De Leon describes the corruption of the plebs and their loss of power after they had compromised with the patricians. Probably Castro has never read De Leon, who would have denounced Castro's lack of doctrine. They have in common a prophetic sense of the leaps in evolution, which appears natural in the light of the common Semitic strain in their temperaments and in their Hispanic culture.

What kind of man is Castro? How can he be pictured, except in his deeds and speeches, which I have seen and related? His character is explicit in his actions. He is not a meditative, not a contemplative man. He likes to have intellectuals around him, but not to discuss ideas so much as to fortify the rightness of his actions with ideas. Although not without culture and mental training, Castro is not therefore an intellectual. The dimension in Marti that inspired his great poems is not active in Castro, although such a speech as *History Will Absolve Me* is a remarkable piece of prose. But in his exquisite sensibilities and responsiveness to every live detail around him, he is less the politician than the poet *and the lover*. This is indeed his mark: that of the passionate but deliberate lover.

He loves Cuba's incompleteness; and the leadership he has won with his colleagues (as distinct from the charisma of his relations with the people) derives from the immediacy, the steel-hard sharpness and the antenna delicacy of his drives and judgments. To call him a "dictator" is dishonest semantics. He writes down in deed what Cuba's needs dictate. But, as he is the most conspicuous Hispano-American leader of our time, he is also the most exposed to jeopardy, from without and within himself. As a man of genius, he of course identifies his self with the substance of his work. But if the identification becomes possessive, he will no longer be the good leader. The great question about Fidel Castro is whether he has enough intellectual detachment to recognize in himself the evils of the lusting ego, which he shares with all men and which might distort his vision and stultify his uses.

His worst mistakes (they are few) seem to derive from what might be called "an absence of mind." Let me give three examples (a more important one will be discussed in the next chapter): (1) His insinuation that the United States was guilty in the explosion of the munition-ship *La Coubre,* in the harbor of Havana, when there was only a vague moral connection between the motives of the presumed act of sabotage and the general hostility of the State department, which probably expresses itself in other forms than blowing up French ships. (2) The "circus" of war-crime trials held in the Sports Palace just after Castro assumed power, and withdrawn almost at once after the case of Jesus Sosa Blanco, who confessed to killing 108 Cubans, when Castro saw the fury of the public. His mind should have foretold the dangerous fury and its remoteness from justice. This early act of Castro gave a pretext to the hostility of the liberal-capitalist world, which was looking for pretexts. (3) The demands that the United States reduce (in forty-eight hours) its embassy staff from over a hundred to eleven—the number of Cubans in the Cuban Embassy at Washington. This was an unreasonable demand. Would it not have been more effective flatly to accuse the United States Embassy of espionage and to ask it to shut its doors, or to postpone all action for a few weeks until the new Kennedy administration had named an envoy perhaps less hostile?

What specific character unifies such varied men? From cosmopolitan lawyers (Dorticos and Castro) to humble soldier of the people (Juan Almeida, the Negro who is chief-of-staff of the armed forces); from radical intellectuals (Roa and Hart) to intuitive man of action (Raul Castro); from trained professionals (Guevara and Faustino Perez[3]) to the chieftains of INRA in the provinces and the cooperative leaders, who must regulate the individual problems of men and women thrust

3. Perez is no longer in the Cabinet.

forward virtually overnight from economic servitude into political and social responsibility? They are all young, they are all passionate patriots: what else characterizes them together?

They differ in background, in race, in intellect and in "know-how." They are improvised agronomists, economists, bankers, buyers, soldiers, leaders of industry and of labor. They are improvised statesmen and diplomats: one might almost say they are improvised *Cubans* in their exalted meaning of the name. Doubtless they make mistakes, for while they act they are still learning. Time will judge their capacities of mind in their perilous undertaking. What composes them together on so many and such complex levels is their sharing, at deep sources of energy unknown to the conventional office-holder, in the immediate work inspired by Cuba's political, industrial and cultural *incompleteness.* Wonderfully surviving the centuries of blood, of piracy (old and new,) and of corruption, the Cubans emerge into history with an experiment—not of mere production, not of mere political independence: an experiment *in goodness.*

Let the fastidious hierophant of freedom (exegetized by American television and Washington news conferences) know what he is opposing!

But Don Quixote also was a good man, whose good deeds became absurd because of his false or inadequate awareness of the world around him; because his mind did not match his good intentions. There is an element in the drama of little Cuba which makes the Knight of La Mancha relevant: the relations of Cuba with the world, particularly the relations of Cuba with the vast United States and with the vast Communist nations. There was also something of Don Quixote in the theoretically correct, the practically lonely Daniel De Leon, something which requires further elucidation.

This romantic reach of America Hispana will come into the next chapter. But the reader should remind himself that these relations with a world, and indeed with the cosmos, are never isolated. They are as ubiquitous as gravitation.

In the final verdict on Cuba's revolution—more precisely on

Cuba's birth—the attitudes of the Cuban leaders toward the world and the attitudes of the world, the Hispano-American and the American world, toward Cuba will reveal much about the future we are creating for ourselves.

This is certain, now: the clock of Cuba's life cannot be set back to what it was. Not to what it was under American possession, not to what it was under Spain. Such survivals of the American domination as the naval base at Guantanamo will disappear, a last vestige of the Platt Amendment. But Cuba's destiny within America Hispana, within the Western Hemisphere, within the world now also rising in Africa, Asia and Europe, rests with the character of the Cubans as it will emerge, made articulate by its leaders.

10. *The Sundered Hemisphere—and Hope*

I

THE following paragraphs are from a book published in 1943[1].

The three Americas (by the third Brazil is meant) have a more immediate possession than a hemisphere; one without which the hemisphere could easily disintegrate, in political and cultural terms, like Africa and Asia. It is their common sense of democratic destiny; their dynamic will that the term New World should have a deeper than the geographic meaning in which the discoverers used it. . . .

Democracy in the complete sense that I have given it must include not only all men but *the whole man.* . . . Short of this wholeness, as our modern history reveals, democracy develops the poisons to destroy itself; freedom employs the energies and genius it has freed to abolish freedom. . . .

Freedom must mean growth not only for all men but for every dimension of man. . . In the complete sense I have given it, democracy is the dominant will, the dominant intuition, of the three Americas. In this universal value, the hemisphere is a new world; the concept of One America has meaning. . . .

The Americas are an island in an overwhelming land-mass; a minority island in the far greater lands and populations of the other hemisphere.

If our island psychology were to generate an economic and military imperialism (there are threats of this), there will be

1. Waldo Frank, *South American Journey* (New York: Duell, Sloan and Pearce, 1943), pp. 364–368.

no hemisphere at all, beyond geography. For our aggressiveness will throw the Hispano-American nations into the hands of whatever power in Europe or Asia or both stands ready to counterpoise us. And in two more generations the immense resources of America Hispana will have torn our hemisphere asunder. . . .

At a meeting of the Organization of American States held in August 1960 at San Jose, Costa Rica, Cuban Chancellor Raul Roa read a list of alleged unfriendly or hostile acts perpetrated against Cuba, for which he placed the blame, directly or indirectly (as issuing from its policy) on the U. S. State Department. Here are some of the particulars of Roa's charges:

1. 1959: Drilling by Cuban counterrevolutionaries protected by local authorities, principally in Florida. Air raids by planes from Florida against Cuba.

2. July 25, 1959: Capture of plane proceeding from Florida, with Rafael del Pino, wanted by the Cuban police.

3. Incendiary bombs dropped on sugar *central* in Pinar del Rio.

4. October 18, 1959: Aerial attack on *central* in Camaguey.

5. October 21, 1959: Bombs over Havana from two planes piloted by two known enemies of the revolution. Two deaths, forty wounded in the Havana streets.

6. October 28, 1959: Second bombing of *central* "Niagara." Magazine *Time* asserts that the plane's base was in southern Florida.

7. October 24, 1959: Bombing of a train in province of Las Villas.

8. January and February, 1960: Almost daily bombings.

9. February 26, 1960: A bombing plane forced down. Its provenance from Florida and the counterrevolutionary character of its personnel and equipment proved beyond doubt.

10. July 12, 1960: Bombing and firing of sugar fields on north coast, near Havana. Also over sugar fields of Las Villas.

11. Attacks by air continue throughout months of 1960.

12. Cancellation of credit to Cuban banks. Freezing of bank accounts. Demand for payment in advance and *in specie* by industrial companies with Cuban relations. Law suits against Cuban airplanes.

13. The legal government of Guatemala, when called on to defend itself against reactionary forces led, as was later divulged, by the American Embassy in Guatemala, had been crippled by the shutting off of the supply of oil to the army. A similar threat existed against Cuba, so long as Venezuelan oil was intercepted and the refineries refused, despite the law, to process government-bought crude oil from the Soviet Union. On this account, as a measure of defense, the refineries had been taken over.

None of these grievances were argued by the Organization of American States. They were not even examined. Instead, the body of Foreign Ministers condemned

> . . . energetically the intervention or threat of intervention, even conditional, by an extra-continental power in the affairs of the American republics and declared that acceptance of intervention from beyond the Continent by an American state endangered the solidarity and security of America,—obliging the Organization of American States to disapprove and to reject it with all energy. . . .

This was, of course, a protest against Cuba's commercial dealings with Communist countries, to which Cuba had been forced (Cuba had no relations with the Soviet Union before 1960) by the now open economic war of the United States and Cuba.

Khruschchev had said:

> We must not forget that the U.S. is no longer at an inaccessible distance from the Soviet Union. Figuratively speaking, if it became necessary, Soviet rockets could defend (or support) the people of Cuba if the aggressive forces of the Pentagon dared to initiate an invasion of Cuba.

By the rules of diplomacy, and of common human nature, Cuba's reception of this assurance was normal—as it was normal for the Thirteen Colonies to accept the active support of the French navy and for the new nations of Bolivar and San Martin to accept the support of the British navy. But the reader will soon see why I disapprove this reasoning. *Standard diplomacy is as obsolete as the weapons on which it relied,* and no nation today dares—even for the sake of justice—to act on its instincts of the jungle, which were adequate when fangs were feeble—or at least were not genocidal. But the ministers at San Jose were acting from no new theory or premise of diplomacy. Simply, the American states were telling their little sister state that when it was threatened by the most powerful of nations it must not accept help, but must consent to be throttled to death in order to preserve the Monroe Doctrine.

The Cuban delegation walked out of the San Jose reunion. Chancellor Roa said:

> The reason which inexorably moves us to this is that despite the declaration and protests here formed to the effect that Cuba could count on the protection and support of the Organization of American States, to which it belongs, against the aggression and intervention of another American State, the proofs here adduced have found no echo, no response, no reception whatsoever. *The Latin American governments have left Cuba in solitude.* . . . I go with my people, and with my people go as well *the peoples* of our America.

On the level of official act, the American Hemisphere seemed sundered.

II

This walkout took place in the last days of August 1960. On September 2, a huge crowd packed the Plaza Civica in Havana.

From the bright new home of the INRA to the monument of Marti, a multitude covered the wide spaces. And Fidel Castro announced, while the crowd roared, that *the crowd* constituted itself "The General National Assembly of the Cuban People." He read what he called "The Declaration of Havana." The crowd roared its affirming vote. Later, it is claimed, 4 million Cubans (over four-sevenths of the population of the island) signed their names to the declaration. It asserted Cuba's independence, political and economic, and Cuba's right to accept the friendship of whatever people offered sincerely to befriend it. No doubts as to that; nor as to the readiness of the San Jose reunion to march in step with the United States.

But let us look a little deeper. Castro has understood the inadequacies and the falsities of elections in parliamentary states, where the choice of candidates is rigged by a system to ensure its own continuance. But Castro must know that a mass meeting also has its limitations. He perhaps has read Gustave Le Bon's *Psychology of Crowds* or Freud's analysis of the individual's regression into the dark unconscious when he becomes part of the crowd, which so readily becomes the mob. Surely he knows that under crowd pressures the individual loses his capacity to ponder, to choose, even to observe.

True democracy, less simple, requires its members to act upon rational resources which no million-headed gathering can produce, although its individuals, with reflection and discussion, can achieve it. A revolution such as Castro's is nourished by the direct, almost physical embrace of leaders and people. In this sense, Fidel Castro is a true tribune. But the leader must never forget that the mass mind is far beneath judgement, self-criticism and detachment. He must keep open the conduits to these, and keep them safe from the people's immediate passion. He must know how to redirect this passion, he must know and dare at times to confront it and oppose it.

For example, to the crowd Khruschchev's notorious "rocket offer" is simple, and they accept it. No nation at any moment can support more than one hate. For the Hindus and the Irish, it was the British; for the Cubans, it is the American government. "Khruschchev's our friend!" they shout. The crowd's image of reality has two sides: the good, Khruschchev and Castro in affectionate embrace; and the bad, Eisenhower in Madrid embracing Franco. But the Cuban leader must reach a deeper reality by asking deeper questions. Is Mr. Khruschchev's statement about the availability of rockets a threat? a promise? a bluff? Would Russia risk atomic war to save Cuba? If so, has Cuba in our present day the right to bring war closer, *even to save itself?* And would war save it? If not, and Khruschchev intends no such war, does not the State Department know it? Who is fooling whom? Are not these antics of an obsolete diplomacy dangerous nonsense?

Let us imagine Castro's answering the rocket proposition of the Russians in words of this order: "We wish to do business with you. We wish to be friends with you. We are grateful for your help in our hour of need. And we are not afraid that business and friendship with you will deflect us from seeking our own way of life, which may not coincide with yours, even as our past within the Judaeo-Christian tradition does not coincide with your past. We know and we respect that if you help us with Russian oil for Cuban sugar, you have your reasons, of benefit to Russia. But under no circumstance will Cuba permit its legitimate needs and rights to precipitate a world war. *We do not want your rockets.* Under no terms will we accept your rockets—or any rockets—which mean death to us all. Our national birth is based upon the love we name when we speak of humanism: the love which is the motive and the incompleted destiny of our revolution. We do not intend to win the right to love and to live by the denial of love and by the threat to life."

No crowd could spontaneously compose such a reply. But the peoples of the crowding globe must learn to find such a reply within themselves—or man must vanish.

What might come of such an answer?

1. The motives moving Russia to help Cuba by buying sugar with oil would not disappear.

2. The world might see that Cuba, transcending insensate nationalism, was trying to act as a member of the human race: a little planet with an orbit of its own (as Raul Roa said), yet a body among others in a common solar system.

3. A wave of understanding might arise, so overwhelming that not alone the rhetorical Russian rocket but the far more real and perilous economic war led by the United States would vanish in a movement of popular approval for the gallant island.

4. The greater consciousness of Cuba might begin to function under conditions more manageable and precise than the whole world scene, which, of course, includes the chaos of Africa and Asia; begin to function within the comparatively coherent and advantageously restricted scene *of the hemisphere,* a name and a place which might again have meaning.

Diplomacy is a nation's face to the reality around it. It should project *the real.* Few nations have, in the history of nations. A vast state can afford a poor (an unreal) diplomacy for a short time, but not for long—and a small people, never. Cuba must articulate unceasingly and shrewdly its relation with reality. But a diplomacy of threat and of reliance on war is as obsolete as bow and arrow. Cuba's strength is its fresh attitude toward individual man and public power. This must be brought to bear with all its light upon its relations with other states—beginning with the United States and America Hispana.

Both a capitalist society such as ours and Communist societies such as the Soviet Union's and China's have been forced by their inner natures to ignore the imperatives of a true diplomacy. The Communist states, in cultures which have known no Renaissance, moved by the urgent need to give the people food and shelter—let us call it social justice—have been encouraged to achieve it by the simplistic means of nationalism, regimentation and police power, which ignored or wounded the needs of *the whole man* (who cannot live by bread alone). The capitalist states, having produced a plenty of food and "things" through the incentive of individual profit, have made the profit motive central and have exalted to power leaders motivated by profit, stultifying the whole man and degrading society into a machine for more production and more profit. Such errors of interpretation of man's nature have been standardized in what is known as diplomatic "Washington," "Downing Street," "Quai d'Orsay" and the "Kremlin." The simplistic psychology of the crowd is exploited in both systems: in the Communist state by demagoguery and censorship, in the capitalist society by the prostitution of the arts, the servile submission of education and the surrender of communications to the mongers of products and profits. *These* have been mirrored in our diplomacy, not the whole man, until the piling up of genocidal weapons—while impotent mannikins parade before the peace-conference tables —becomes a terrible symbol.

The way of Cuba must transcend both systems, which tend to pool their distinctive features until they sink together into a herd of intellectual, emotional and spiritual dwarfs. As I have pointed out elsewhere, many nations have had prophets: the difference of the Jews was that they obeyed and incorporated their prophets. Cuba, whose great prophet is Jose Marti, must do likewise. This means a long road before Cuba (and before man), but no other will save Cuba (or save man), even if the bombs are all safely disposed of. The road leads into difficult jungles and forbidding heights. And the simplicities of the crowd must not be lost, for there lies the energy and the intuitive insight. But there must be, *from the beginning*, awareness of the complexities of the true road and studies of how to take it.

As we have seen, much has been done already. The land of Cuba, and the works thereof, have been returned, at least formally, to the people. The great producing agents—factories, refineries, mines—have been wrested from foreign powers supremely indifferent to the plight of Cuba's people and exclusively concerned with profit. The schools have become intellectually productive, and all these agents of integration by nationalization have been theoretically placed in the hands of the people. They have yet to learn that nationalization is not enough; that they will not really possess their land until they relate each producing unit to all, and all to their condition as members of an organism of peoples. The youth of Cuba has been awakened to values within them and beyond the individual ego, although this, too, is a mere threshold of the far more complex problems of the collective ego. Politics, not to go wrong, must be related to psychology, and psychology to the person: to the rediscovery of the person. There must be a return to the self, an *education* of the self, not imagined today in such crude ideologies as the orthodox materialism of the Communists or the orthodox rationalism of the capitalists or the nationalisms now rampant in many parts of the world.

Only the future can tell the permanence of these reforms in Cuba. (But what *we* are and do decides the future.)

III

One day in late October 1960, a tall, impeccably dressed black man stepped from the plane at the Havana airport, accompanied by Foreign Minister Raul Roa; and was warmly welcomed by President Dorticos, Premier Castro and other high officials. In the cultured French of Paris he assured them that he and his people and all Africans were devoted to the cause of Cuba. This was Sekou Toure, President of the Republic of Guinea, once a colony of France. His alliance with Cuba is a symbol of the swift events that moved Antonio Nuñez Jimenez, director of INRA, to say to me in quiet confidence: "Hemisphere? Hemisphere solidarity? That is all finished. Twenty years ago, perhaps, the term had meaning still. Not today."

To the *conquistadores* and the first settlers, the term New World meant a land unit in geography, as it appeared *to* Europe and *from* Europe. To the seventeenth-century zealots of New

England, it meant the New Jerusalem and Zion, strictly bounded by the European doctrine of each sect. We have seen that to the first American statesmen, beginning with Jefferson and Madison, it meant a new world along the lines and limits of eighteenth-century Anglo-Saxon thought. To the Spanish monarchs from Isabella down, it was merely a new part of an old world, built by eternity on the rock of St. Peter—an old world to be geographically completed by simple addition.

Bolivar had precursors (Francisco de Miranda, for one) in his vision of a hemisphere as the lay "city of God," whose justice and peace would be in global contrast to the old world of misery. Toward this beginning, he convoked his Congress of Panama and promised the Isthmus of Panama (Colombian territory) as hemisphere capital, where all the Americas would deliberate together at the side of an inter-American canal. But it was William Blake and the nineteenth-century poets, captained by Walt Whitman, who most articulately saw "the new world" as a new vision.

Meantime, another unity was being imposed upon the hemisphere: the unity of the Monroe Doctrine, whose sole active builder, as we have seen, was the United States, a unity of economic organization visible in such works as the anarchic oil towns of Mexico, the banana fields of the United Fruit Company in Central America, the mining camps of Anaconda in Chile. This passive unity, imposed by the North, was of course being constantly disturbed by the growth of the Hispanic republics. Mexico's revolution of 1910 was a blow against it. Remote, rich nations such as Brazil and Argentina never wholly succumbed to it. The speed of modern communications decomposed it. Already by the turn of the twentieth century, the notion of all America as a new world could thrive only in so far as the ideal of a new City of Man endowed it. The New World, which meant nothing but a geographical term to Amerigo Vespucci, now meant nothing except in the domain of the ideal.

The ideal could have thrived, if it had been encouraged by the brains and nervous system of the economic unity. If there had been in our businessmen and politicians a sincere conviction that other ways of life might be as good as their own, and an acceptance that the growth of the American nations, including our own, required basic readjustments in the American ways of life, the term "hemisphere" might have recaptured meaning. We have seen in Cuba, in the regimes of Machado and Batista, extreme examples of the facts. Complacency and arrogance followed the American flag. The poets, in verse and prose, lived in a "new world" of the ideal, while the hemisphere was worked as if it were a North American plantation. The nations of Europe, not sympathetic but recognizing power, tacitly concurred.

Cuba with Castro (this is the meaning of his strength) has fulfilled rather than *caused* the end of that era. The State Department's cold hostilities, seconded by the liberals whose fears of basic change make them partners of the reactionaries, have finally forced Cuba into close economic intercourse—and, cultural will follow—with Russia and the Far East. In vain will the other governments of America Hispana resist the same trend in their peoples. The affirmative support of Castro by Mexico's greatest political leader since Juarez, former President Lazaro Cardenas, recognizes what is bound to be, because it exists already. Meanwhile, the past colonial experiences of the new African nations give them a basis of empathy with Cuba—wireless and airplane helping—an empathy which cuts across hemisphere lines, dissolving them.

In the days of Jefferson and John Quincy Adams, despite the hidden will-to-power of the Monroe Doctrine, there was meaning to the political alignment of all the American republics together in defensive stance against France, Britain, Spain and Holland, which were all still comparatively strong. Only their constant bickerings saved the new nations, which had a common ground of self-protection. (It was this need of distance from strong neighbors, rather than the land, which inspired Jefferson in the Louisiana Purchase.) All these motives and conditions are gone. Only a rediscovered value in viable, contemporary terms—valid in the United States no less than in America Hispana—could re-endow the hemisphere with meaning.

What do all the American peoples have in common? Is there something they dare not lose because it would mean a loss of self, something whose survival and nurture demands the support of all our resources, all our genius?

IV

Under all, there is a psychological factor. All Americans, except our Indians, share the experience of being recent arrivals. Asians, Africans and Europeans, too, were settlers after great migrations, but they have been where they are for a long time. Their memories of past homes have been expunged—and their sense of guilt, if it ever existed, of how they got their new homes. The farmer of Iowa, the gaucho of Argentina's pampa, the subway-riding immigrant from Italy and Poland, the Brazilian whose grandfather was born in Portugal, Holland or Japan . . . share with the Negro descended from slaves the experience of a world literally new. This experience subtly infuses their nerves, their minds, their arts and their language—even infuses, with their food, the metabolism of their bodies. On the contrary, the Europeans, the Africans and the Asians have in common the feel for their earth as home, a feeling which in Americans is split to include the earth they have abandoned.

Of course, the old world also had its conquered and annihilated cultures: in India, the Dravidians; in Rome, the Etruscans; in Israel, the Canaanites. But long ages have completed their absorption, or rationalized their differences, as in the case of the East Indians. There is no sense of guilt left, such as the common although unconscious feeling of the Americans toward their predecessors. The basic cause of this guilt is a treasure shared by us all: the Yankee with three centuries in New England, the pants-making Jew born in the Ukraine and living in Brooklyn, the verse-writing *caballero* of Bogota, the illiterate tin-miner of Bolivian Potosi, the liberal graduate of Radcliffe College and the militia girl in Cuba. That treasure is our sense of the individual, *our value of the person.* Every American (except the Indian) feels it, and through it feels guilt in his possession of a home which meant the dispossession of another.

True, the treasure of our sense of the person is more honored in the breach than in the observance. The Madison Avenue go-getter may confuse it with the acquisition of gadgets; the up-to-date technician may sneer at its source, the Bible, the white-supremacy segregationist may deny it in his brother, the Negro; and the radical may unwittingly reject it by his espousal of a vulgar Marxism whose premise conceives the individual as primarily a product of economics. Nevertheless, we of America all have it.

Our value of the person is not universally shared. Far from it! And one can call it innate only because it is a potential all men may strive for and because no strictly *new* element can be added to an organism. Certain philosophies of the West declare it to be doomed.[2] The great religions of the East, of India and China, explicitly deny it. All attitudes toward Nature and the real nature of man are to be found in the rich philosophies of the East. But the dominant ones, originally from India, repudiate nature and the individual, hitching "salvation" to knowledge of their nonexistence. China either adopts the Hindu view or relegates the individual to a contingent factor of family or the group, which becomes the true integer, the exclusive source of man's true values.[3] A modulation of classical Chinese values, beginning even before Confucius, readily leads to the Communist doctrine which also makes man contingent upon

2. See the Marxist philosophers. Also Roderick Seidenberg, *Post-historic Man* (Chapel Hill: Univ. of North Carolina, 1950).

3. For the development of this theme see Waldo Frank, *The Rediscovery of Man.*

mass, denying in the individual that cosmic dimension or direct conduit to God, which is the fundamental law of the Judaeo-Christian Tradition. This concurrence of Chinese with Communist thought must be understood to understand Communist China, even as the fervid nationalism into which the Marxist collective ego may modulate must be understood to understand Communist Russia. It was the sense of the immediacy of God within the person that inspired the Renaissance in Western and Central Europe. Russia and the East had no equivalent of either Renaissance or Reformation.

Our democratic doctrine and faith issue directly from this Western sense of man's nature. In the vast majority of the world, the nations are not rooted in our premise of what man *is*. Even when they call themselves "peoples' democracies," they give the words a narrower and shallower content, stressing equality, not freedom.

Here then is the key to a new revaluation and revival of the hemisphere. With Western Europe (a mere nub of the huge land mass of Eurasia), we uphold—uphold alone—our sense of man, within and *against* a world vastly more populous. We are a minority, even if Western Europe remains with us. But minorities can conquer, *with a truth*. Witness Israel and Greece.[4]

Only the American republics, from their birth as nations, were consciously and deliberately rooted in the democratic Judaeo-Christian vision of the whole man. But they lack method, law and economic structure to actualize this vision and this love. And while they grope, they must fight the denial of their axiom in a majority world: a majority abroad and a majority at home, in the practice of our economic system. No easy task. And viable only if the American nations gather their strengths and achieve the harmony of common purpose. If we betray that purpose—even with fine words, as official American business (the State Department) has betrayed it in Cuba—there is no hope for us.

4. The theme of our *Atlantic World* was first developed in my *America Hispana: A Portrait and a Prospect* (New York: Scribner, 1931).

V

As I write and this is read, there lie in the arsenals of the United States, the Soviet Union, Britain and France enough hydrogen bombs to wipe life from this earth. This is one peril we must live with; perhaps until one nation proves itself sane by unilateral action, and with the world's people behind it, leads the other nuclear nations to sanity. (Wisdom always seems unilateral at first.)

But of equal peril to man is his alienation from self-knowledge, and it is this that has converted the machine from an instrument of human welfare into a monster of the collective ego. The products of science have given us the power to destroy man. Now man must achieve the knowledge and the organ to save himself. This is a crisis known to evolution. The environment changes; the creature must change or vanish. The fish transmutes its fins to legs, its gills to lungs; the reptile becomes a bird and leaps into the air. The leap is the creativity of nature; the orgasmic poem that adds a new unit to the universe. Man, threatened by the jungle of the machines, which have become his environment, must leap to safety.

Cuba has shown it is not afraid to leap. But far more is expected of Cuba than the ownership of its fields and factories, which we might call "the little leap of breakfast." The reader knows what breakfast means to those who have slept hungry. Let no man who has eaten minimize the importance of breakfast for those who have not had it. Shall we help Cuba to the little leap and over, or do our worst (as we are doing) to keep it hungry? But Cuba, too, must gain perspective "beyond breakfast" or risk the distortion of its good intentions.

Cuba, we have seen, has been the victim of evil in many forms, for a long time. And it is right to hate evil. But hate which oversimplifies and becomes hate of the perhaps unconscious evil-doer, like mere resistance to evil, cannot overcome evil. Hate must be transcended by a positive good, and the one good is love.

Love has been the strength of Castro and his company. Now the State Department declares its war against Cuba. Castro and his fellows must not let this evil deflect or shrink their love. It is going to be hard for the Cuban people not to hate. They must go on knowing that among the victims of the American system, of "things for profit," the most deeply infected and endangered are ourselves of the United States. We are all victims, the Cuban leaders must stress; we are all urgent candidates for the leap of recreation. Observing man in both societies, capitalist and Communist, Cuba must know that they converge toward the same lobotomized mass man; that if they do not blow each other up first, they will meet and become one—unless a deeper vision replaces them both.

Cuba, a little country cast for a great role, too often speaks offensive-defensively; as if it were so conscious that it is smaller, it dares talk only as if it were bigger.

Here's an example. The liberals in the United States voice their regret that Cuba has made no public move (despite Castro's early promises) to hold elections. Cuba could explain that in the present state of virtual war, elections would encourage sabotage and sedition under the guise of electioneering. At the speed Cuba is going, the break of elections would have the shattering effect of thrusting a motor at 100 miles per hour into "first." Surely, Castro says to himself, this is obvious to people of good will and intelligence. Nevertheless, Castro should be humble enough to plan elections for the future when the state of self-defensive war has lifted. Another example: the evaporation of the dissident press. Every honest visitor to Cuba knows that the revolution has produced a climate of such passionate devotion and work that a reactionary press shrivels, spontaneously, in it. Cuba should subvene a dissenting press; it should advertise its sense of the difference between sedition (the enemy it must put down) and dissenting discourse (which might aid it in self-knowledge.)

Recently I was discussing these problems with an intelligent seventeen-year-old American schoolgirl, who made an observation amazingly acute. "If," she said, "the heat of battle in Cuba's state of war requires censorship, if it requires that elections be postponed and political foes sequestered, why does not the government publish a *prospective Bill of Rights* making clear Cuba's intention to guarantee, as soon as feasible, minority opinion, a free press and free elections?" We reminded each other that a dozen years after their Declaration of Independence the Thirteen Colonies judged themselves ready for elections, and that the suspension of certain civil rights is a concomitant of every war. And I reminded myself that this generous and eager girl (so close to the youth who are operating Cuba) was quite as much *an American* as the high-pressure salesman or the State Department that protects him.

In the profound evaluation of man's whole nature, which must be the matrix of Cuba's birth, Cuba's ally is the religious tradition of the American people—even if they sin against Cuba. Cuba's adversary is the Communists' and businessmen's shallow sense of man—even if they help by swapping oil for sugar.

VI

On the south shore of Cuba, west of Cienfuegos, very close to the Bay where the American authorities staged their invasion of April 1961, there is a vast swamp, the Peninsula and Cienaga of Zapata, with a broad lagoon known as *"el Tesoro,"* "the Treasure." Columbus saw this nebula of earth-mist-water, and steered clear of it. Until the revolution, it remained a waste, without road or settlement, wholly possessed by the long-legged water birds, the reptiles and the myriads of insects. It is a green-gray domain which the sun can never brighten, because of the haze of water it draws in suspense between the sun's rays and the water. Part of chaos, it seems, of pre-Creation, of the nameless and formless void from which Jehovah made the firmaments. Its water is not-water, its earth is not-earth, its day is not-day. And it appears to have lain nebulous forever, in a state not of creation but of incompletion, and in potential fabulously fertile.

Now the engineers of INRA are draining the huge swamp. As the waters sink from the muck, straight roads of reddish earth appear, and little rivers of sweet water, and fresh springs. A land emerges. And as we approach it from the air, we see fields of rice flowing in cool liquid emerald waves under the sun and orderly acres of tomatoes. The cooperative we aim at has an air strip. Not the most primitive conveyance could reach it: not a rowboat, not a team of oxen, only the plane. As we dip and straighten for the run, nearing the group of houses we see a set of scarlet bugs: huge tomatoes. Finally we recognize a little fleet of helicopters. We halt, and the tomato growers, men, women and children, who are not at work out in the fields, race up and greet us warmly—Castro, Nuñez Jimenez, others—but casual as if they were familiar and as if their meeting in a swamp, a score of miles away from habitable Cuba, were as common as the meeting of neighbors round the village pump of any Cuban hamlet. As in other remote parts of the island, they got used to Castro's dropping in when he has a day to spare. He loves this swamp because he destines it to be a Nile of Cuba, a huge provider of rice and cotton, and no less to be a paradise for fishermen and hunters.

After the inevitable parley about something, something Fidel *must* hear, we scramble into the helicopters which spin their lanky arms, gaining speed until they rise, shifting from shoulder to shoulder like Pegasus with invisible wings. We swoop low over the tomato fields, our salute to the waving workers almost as close as handshake. We follow a partly cut road, whirling past a squad of men at work on it; and rise to a full view of the lagoon on whose edge stands alone a grey-roofed, white-wood structure. Raised planks over the wet shore, making a narrow boardwalk, lead to it from the water where a couple of row-boats lie, and our helicopter lands beside the cottage on a square spot just big enough and dry enough to hold it. The house, which Castro and his friends take over from time to time for a day's fishing (and sleep), is the headquarters of the drainage engineers. There's a long room with a dozen bunks in double tiers. There's a small air-conditioned bedroom for a couple (Raul and Vilma Castro will have it tonight) and a neat little kitchen with a gas refrigerator, where someone is always being fed by Celia or Lupe or Vilma. Castro invites me to go fishing; we sit silent in the dory and get never a bite. Near us on the shaky little wharf Raul Corrales (excellent photographer) pulls out a fat carp, which he brandishes gloatingly before Castro's eyes. Fidel makes up a comic scene: there's a "conspiracy" against him! This kind of fooling is frequent. The general tone is of ease and relaxation. Everyone of the dozen or more making up the party (including the armed boy guards) does what he wants, says what he wants—or so it seems—and eats and sleeps when he wants.

The night is the time for talk as a serious undertaking. The mood reminds me of jam sessions at college, although the topics could not differ more. These are young men and women, sparkling with animal spirits. The veterans go over an event in the Sierra Maestra: a question of tactics and of who did what in that already historic time; or argue how a situation should be met in a new cooperative store in Camaguey. Always they disagree, reminding me less of college men than of any gathering in Israel where, as to detail, there will always be as many opinions as there are individuals present.

I recall that this doubtless domineering man is called a dictator, even a Communist dictator. It seems unreal. Perhaps the name needs redefining.

At midnight I am exhausted and hungry for sleep. I pitch into the bunk farthest from where the men are smoking, eating and drinking *malta*. Malta is the near-beer which is the closest to alcohol Castro approves of—except when he orders wine for a friend at dinner in some Havana restaurant and sips a glass politely. Alone, he is more likely to eat with his comrades in the kitchen. In their forever talking, they remind me more and more of the Irish (who inhabited another island close to the power that oppressed.) Good sweet talkers, both the Irish and the Cubans, whose Spanish at times seems as remote from the Castilian as Gaelic from English.

Two or three of the bunks are already occupied, one by one of the women. It's been a strenuous day, and I fall asleep at once. . . . As suddenly I am waked from deep slumber. I look at my watch: 3 A.M. From the air-cooled room, with the door open, comes a prolific shouting. Angry (my nerves jangle when I am sharply disturbed in sleep), and only half awake (a bad combination), I climb down from my bunk and go to the room where they are squatting and shouting and having a good time. "It's not easy to sleep," say I, "in such an explosion!" I can see them seeing me: the old man who needs his sleep, the good-hearted Yankee. They're sorry to have disturbed me; they're feeling a bit sheepish. Now as I climb back into bed the house is so still I hear the night birds shriek and the fugue-like percussion of the frogs.

When I awake with the day already large and steaming, I realize that I have been rude, and have rebuked Castro! I'm ready to apologize; but Castro is sleeping in one of the bunks; and when, hours later, he awakes, apology or even mention of the matter seems inept. If it is brought up, it must be in a jest by Castro. And I realize suddenly that I do not know his feeling. The little event has sunk into a realm of reserve, where I will never enter.

As we ride together in the globed red helicopter that seems to brush the land, plain or sierra, with intimate touch and yet remains aloof, I am aware that this man's hands are the sensitive hands of an artist, perhaps of a sculptor modeling from life. I am aware that his quickened receptivities, far beyond the normal, are the nerve-process of the artist. And is not every artist—assembling his material, ruthlessly rejecting, selecting, finally shaping it to form—in a way a dictator? In the absorptive creativity of Castro's leadership, with its swift intuitive resolutions that from the outside seem to be arbitrary, there are surely elements to suggest the term "dictator," as there were in Bolivar and in wartime Lincoln. Any strong and creative executive in war, when civil rights are suspended, to the extent that his intuitions override rational counsel, will be called at times "dictator." But to join Lincoln, De Gaulle or Castro with the family of Franco, Mussolini, Hitler, the dwarf Trujillos and Perons of America Hispana, is to insult the language. The term dictator should be reserved for those who *destroy or stultify their people in order to rule;* not sleazily applied to the awakeners of their people, to the creators of their people.

Nevertheless, strong men, creative men in politics, present a danger. It was because our Constitutional fathers realized this that they built checks and balances *against* the executive power. This is the political genius of the Anglo-Saxons: the curb on *strong leaders* which is a prerequisite of a democracy that *works.* And it must be said beyond cavil that the Hispanic people have not shown much of this genius, since the last Spanish master of absolute executive power without balance or check, Felipe II. Absolute executive power, even when won, as in Castro's case, by the bestowal of the people and the benevolent gifts of the man, is a danger. But war also is a danger, especially victorious war. Indeed, war is so acute a danger to the autonomy of a people that even the Anglo-Saxon nations, despite their genius for balances, fall into virtual dictatorship in wartime.

Moreover, every war (and Castro is waging daily war for survival) is ugly. Even a just war is ugly. If the liberal refuses all war, because he is opposed to all injustice and all violence, let him rally to his Christian pacifism, and God be with him. We shall respect him. But if he accepts the premise that war is permissible for winning the independence and freedom of a people; if he accepts our American Revolution, our Civil War, the wars against Hitler; then his opposition to the inevitable tactics of Cuba's war becomes suspect. Insincerity, stupidity, or ignorance must lie behind it. Let the liberal realize the handicap of the men of Hispanic culture: their political inexperience. Let him realize that the cooperative farm, for all its risk of regimenting the peasant, could develop into a form of syndicalist democracy far more fitted to the Hispanic nature and to human need than the crude state farms of Russia, and the present liberal opposition will cease to be sterile.[5]

Peril is always inherent in greatness, and we are not blind to the perils in Fidel Castro's movement. He is a true leader and the people learned to love him. But even if he studied the means of establishing balances in Cuba's government against the overbearing strength of executive power (which has long been the Hispanic political pattern: strong authority—revolt against it—strong authority again), could he institute a change so basic in his own person, having created the myth of his present methods? And can he live forever? Does not his very presence and power impede the constitutional establishment of checks and balances to the excess he represents? What if the people at the moment love Fidel and his bearded *rebeldes* and his smooth-faced *milicianos* more than they love a guarantee of constitutional freedom?

Even this suggestion calls for antithesis. These men and women achieving hope in the abysmal swamp of Zapata, because they are in love with Cuba's *incompletion,* must not be judged wholly as *a promise for tomorrow.* Their worth is immediate and intrinsic. They must be accepted and loved for what they are *today.* A work of art is *itself* and our absorption of it does not hinge on what it may be or may do tomorrow. The manifestation of Cuba's life *today* has the immediacy of beauty and the works of love. Tomorrow, these men and women may be overcome; the cold hate of the capitalist world, whose head is the State Department of the United States, may destroy them—or their own weaknesses and errors may destroy them. What they are, and what they are doing, and what Cuba through them *is* in incompletion, have timeless and independent value.

5. See Appendix 4.

It is significant that in judging Castro's Cuba, the word "sin" comes to mind. If the government of the United States stifles Cuba and betrays America Hispana, it *sins*. If the Hispanic states abandon Cuba to its foes, America Hispana *sins*. If Cuba's revolution of social justice forgets that the mother of justice is love, and when the mother dies justice withers and turns monster, Cuba *sins*, falling short of its high birth. Sin today is an unpopular word—for cause. For it holds a profound truth: the linkage of the person with the world and with cosmos. The first truth implicit in our "sinning" is that we are responsible to others: each of us, we are our brother's keeper. The second truth about sin is that everyone sins; sin is omnipresent. All history is the record of man's failure not to sin. And the final truth of sin is that those who are of good will and good faith are forgiven.

Consciousness of what the Cubans are today must become the premise of American collaboration in what the Cubans are doing.

Postscript
Communism and the Psychology of War

THERE was nothing essentially new in the armed assault on Cuba of April 1961. It was predictable, and it was predicted: both the attack and the fiasco. As the reader knows, it has been in the nature of American government since Jefferson and Clay to covet Cuba for profit and for power. And it was in the nature of the American people, once they had seen photographs of starving Cuban children, to wish Cuba to be free. This conflict of wills explains why we bungled the invasion. Our hand was not firm; our resolution was not resolute. Our State Department is the guardian of American property rights abroad; but also it seeks to uphold the American tradition of liberty for all. The two motives get tangled and stultify one another.

The Soviet Union does better when it invades, for its idealism is 100 per cent absorbed by the dialectical materialism of its politics of power. Britain in its age of imperialist expansion did better, having erected a wall hermetically closed between its cruel deeds abroad and its "sportsmanship" at home. But never fear. When the confusion of conflict begins sorely to hurt us, we'll settle in favor of political egoism, and let the libertarians shift for themselves. This means that Cuba—the creative Cuba we have portrayed—is still in mortal danger.

Even earlier than the embargoes and boycotts, we set the stage for what has occurred. We so acted as to offer Cuba the alternatives: starve or do business with Russia. And we threw

1. Castro told me that, until the sugar and oil restrictions by the U.S., there had not been so much as an exchange of letters between the Cuban and Russian governments.

up our hands in pious horror when the Cubans failed to choose starvation rather than offend our Monroe Doctrine.[1] We forced Cuba to be free—or cease to exist.

Cuba's was an authentic American revolution, *and it still is*. We forced it into relations with Russia: economic and political, with the cultural to follow. But there is not the slightest evidence that Cuba's cordial relations with Russia, China, *et al.*, commit it to give up its passionate need of nationhood or to join any bloc or party line. There *is* danger that subtle political and cultural pressures, alien to the Hispano-American ethos, will play on Cuba; that men in touch with Russia (including, of course, the Communist party) will win undue influence in Cuba simply because the Soviets helped Cuba in its need. Above all, there is immense danger that the state of perpetual defense against possible attack, which we are forcing upon Cuba, will harden Cuba into the authoritarian and totalitarian forms that war and defense against war ineluctably require.

Of course we could openly crush Cuba—any day. If we do, we stand before the entire world (including ourselves) shamed, feared and hated. This and our divided conscience will probably deter us, even more than the possible responses from Moscow. But if we compel Cuba to devote all its resources and energies to defense, we cripple the chances of democracy in Cuba. How did Stalin come to power? It is true that Russia had no tradition of personal freedom, such as that of America Hispana. But did not the five armies from capitalist countries that invaded Russia and tried to kill its revolution help to produce the atmosphere of hate, suspicion, crisis, cunning and desperate defense that Stalin represented? A Cuba in perpetual expectation of attack, direct or indirect, will inevitably take on traits of totalitarian regimentation under whatever home—as will the U.S.A. if it is threatened.

The Cubans on their island have begun to create a generous world. I have experienced it, and it is lovable. It is a world in close harmony with the needs of people everywhere. And this empathy is part of Cuba's strength. But it cannot flower and it cannot last if it must indefinitely continue to breathe within the perpetual vise of military mobilization. This new world, to thrive, needs freedom, relaxation, competition, the infinite variants and airs of play, leisure and love; and also it needs the strict disciplines of the arts and the ethics of peace in order to apply its just laws. We have seen wonderful beginnings in Cuba! They can not go on in a climate of fear, of defense, and of the shutting out of all else. Athens could shrink and rigidify into Sparta.

The day—if it must be—of Cuba's succumbing to the antidemocratic forces within the psychology of war will be no victory for the United States. We, too, shall have become the victims of a corrupt authoritarianism, of economic and intellectual regimentation, of all the false simplifications of a culture of war and of preparation for war. We, too, shall have lost the flexibilities and fluencies of freedom. For we, too, will be threatened by our threat.

Cuba's only hope is our own hope: a change of attitude and course, based on the true nature of the American people, which is generous, expressed by a new leadership.

The end

Appendix 1
A Chronology of the First Years after Castro's Coming to Power

1959

Jan. 1 After twenty-five months of civil war, Batista flees from Cuba.

Jan. 4 Manuel Urrutia Lleo named Provisional President.

Jan. 7 U.S. recognizes government of Cuba.

Jan. 10 Earl T. Smith, U.S. Ambassador, resigns. Accused of helping Batista. Philip Bonsal succeeds him.

Jan. 21 Half a million people in Havana demand shooting of war criminals.

Jan. 23 Castro goes to Venezuela, to help celebrate first anniversary of overthrow of Perez Jimenez. Admiral Wolfgang Larrazabel declares: "If Cuba is attacked, we will defend her."

Jan. 27 Dulles announces withdrawal of U.S. Army mission. Sports Palace open trial of Jesus Sosa Blanco, accused of 118 murders. Fury of crowd frightens Castro who discontinues open trials. Sosa retried in court. U.S. press campaign begins against Castro, because of execution of war criminals.

Feb. 2 Assassination attempt against Castro.

Feb. 16 Jose Miro Cardona replaced by Castro as Premier.

Mar. 3 Government "intervenes" with Cuban Telephone Company; lowers phone rates.

Mar. 6 Rents reduced by as much as 50 per cent.

Mar. 23 U.S. State Department, in reply to protests of Cuban government, declares it has no evidence of preparation on its territory of any invasion of Cuba.

Apr. 15 Castro visits U.S. on "unofficial" good will visit. Meetings with editors, congressmen, *et al.;* but not with President Eisenhower. Castro in New York's Central Park addresses 35,000. Man with bomb arrested. Castro proceeds to Toronto. Disclaims any part by Cubans in Panama revolution.

May 2 Before Committee of Twenty-one, assembled in Buenos Aires, Castro suggests $30 billion to solve Latin America's underdeveloped economic problem. Committee disbands because of insufficient agreement, and Castro withdraws his $30 billion project.

May 17 In the Sierra Maestra, Castro affirms Agrarian Reform law, making illegal the ownership of more than thirty *caballerias* of land. The *latifundio* is abolished (1 caballeria equals 33½ acres).

June 3 Agrarian Reform law in effect.

June 11 Raul Roa replaces Roberto Agramonte as Chancellor.

June 12 Ernesto Guevara begins three months' tour of Africa, Southeast Asia and Europe.

June 17 Venezuela and Cuba denounce in Organization of American States plot by Dominican Dictator Trujillo against both countries.

June 23 Many Cuban *latifundios* expropriated.

June 25 Twenty-five expeditionists from Nicaragua, about to invade Cuba, intercepted on the high seas.

June 26 Cuba breaks off diplomatic relations with Dominican Republic.

June 30 Commandante Pedro Luis Diaz Lanz, head of Cuba's air force, deserts.

July 13 U.S. Senate subcommittee for internal security in Washington hears accusations of Lanz that Cuba is in Communist hands. He also testifies before the FBI. Batista applies to U.S. for permission to enter.

July 17 Castro resigns as Premier; accuses Urrutia Lleo of

holding up revolutionary action. General strike in support of Castro.

July 18 Council of Ministers accepts Lleo's resignation. Osvaldo Dorticos replaces him as President of Republic. Previously, Dorticos had been Minister of Revolutionary Laws. Before gathering of half a million, Castro withdraws his resignation as Premier. Lazaro Cardenas, former President of Mexico, under whom Mexican oil was nationalized, is present at this meeting.

Aug. 3 Cuba decides to attend meeting of Foreign Ministers in Chile.

Aug. 10 Vast plot uncovered against revolution, led by association of large cattle owners.

Aug. 13 Plot of air invasion, proceeding from Dominican Republic, uncovered in Trinidad.

Aug. 14 Castro declares he will not attend Chile meeting of Foreign Ministers, which he characterizes as "a farce." Roa's life threatened.

Aug. 29 Cuban Embassy in Haiti closed; Ambassador recalled.

Sept. 7 Batista arrives in Madeira (Portuguese).

Sept. 8 Trujillo enlists mercenaries for attack on Cuba.

Sept. 18 Roa denies accusation of U.S. Admiral Arleigh Burke that Soviet submarines have been identified in Cuban waters.

Sept. 24 Roa in UN reiterates his appeal for $30 billion to overcome economic underdevelopment in Latin America.

Sept. 26 Argentine Foreign Minister Diogenes Taboada arrives in Cuba on three days' official visit.

Sept. 30 In response to U.S. repudiation of its Cuban sugar quota, Cuba sells 3,330,000 tons of sugar to Soviet Union.

Oct. 8 Cuba reiterates its protest of clandestine flights over Cuba by planes based in U.S.

Oct. 11   Ignacio Luis Arcaya, Venezuelan Chancellor, arrives on official visit.

Oct. 17   Cuba protests U.S. opposition to Cuba's purchase of planes in England.

Oct. 18   Former left-wing President of Guatemala, Juan Jose Arevalo, arrives in Cuba.

Oct. 21   Air attacks on Havana. Two killed, forty-five wounded.

Oct. 22   U.S. announces it will investigate the attacks. Militia of Cuban youth is formed: workers, peasants and students of both sexes.

Oct. 27   U.S. protests Agrarian Reform laws' treatment of U.S. property rights in interview between U.S. Ambassador and President Dorticos, who defends the legal actions.

Oct. 28   Camilo Cienfuegos lost in flight from Camaguey to Havana.

Oct. 30   U.S. authorities confiscate plane which bombed Havana, with forty-seven victims.

Nov. 11   Cuba in UN supports effort to prevent atomic trials by France in Sahara.

Nov. 12   Roa in note deplores worsening U.S.-Cuban relations.

Nov. 24   Archbishop of Havana, Msgr. Evelio Diaz, denies that church property has been confiscated by the government.

Nov. 26   Ernesto Guevara named president of Bank of Cuba.

Nov. 28   National Catholic Congress closes.

Dec. 3   Cuba suggests congress of underdeveloped countries to meet in Havana in 1960.
Cuba protests U.S. action in preventing British sales of fifteen combat planes to Cuba.

Dec. 9   Youth Congress scheduled to take place in Havana.

Dec. 15   Cuban War Tribunal sentences ex-Major Huberto Matos to twenty years' imprisonment.

1960

Jan. 2   Chancellor Roa begins Afro-Asian tour.

Jan. 4   Castro leads 400 university students up Pico Turquino in Sierra Maestra—highest Cuban mountain, where rebellion against Batista began. Asks extradition from U.S. of Diaz Lanz, former air chief, who had admitted participation in aerial attack on Havana.

Jan. 11   Castro hands over to Minister of Education Armando Hart the "Fifth Station of Police" to be converted into a school. "Not a barracks will remain," he declares.

Jan. 21   Sugar harvest for 1960 fixed at 5.5 million tons.

Jan. 23   Pope receives Chancellor Roa and expresses hope that social economic revolution in Cuba will prosper.

Jan. 25   Castro grants 300 property titles to peasants in Pinar del Rio.

Jan. 26   President Eisenhower denies "aggressive intent" and declares U.S. will not interfere in Cuba's internal affairs.

Jan. 28   Moncada Barracks in Santiago become a school. Planes based on Florida ignite many sugar fields in Cuban provinces.

Jan. 30   Castro declares death penalty for misappropriators of public funds.

Feb. 3   Havana airport taken over by government.

Feb. 4   Vice-Premier Mikoyan of Soviet Union arrives in Havana to inaugurate Soviet Exhibition.

Feb. 6   Soviet Russia buys 345,000 tons of Cuban sugar. Commercial treaty (principally oil for sugar) signed with Russia. Cuba receives credit of $100 million; 5 million tons of sugar and other primary goods to be bought within period of five years.

Feb. 29   Herbert Matthews of *New York Times* declares Cuban revolution is not Communist but nationalist.

Mar.	4	Explosion in Havana Harbor of French vessel, *La Coubre*, loaded with ammunition. It is ascertained by experts that the cause was internal. One hundred dead, two hundred wounded. Castro in his funeral oration puts "moral" blame on U.S. anti-Cuban agitation.
Mar.	18	Thirty-four million dollars granted to 400 cooperatives in sugar production.
Mar.	24	Red China buys 80,000 tons of Cuban sugar.
Mar.	26	Brazilian candidate for President (now President) Janio Quadros visits Cuba.
Apr.	1	Venezuela and Cuba sign commercial pact.
Apr.	5	British Guiana and Cuba sign trade pact.
Apr.	22	Japan and Cuba sign trade pact with minimum of 450,000 tons of sugar.
May	1	Castro declares U.S. is preparing aggression against Cuba, via Guatemala; also from the naval base of Guantanamo.
May	7	Diplomatic relations established with Soviet Union. Visit of President Ahmend Sukarno of Indonesia. INRA takes over thousands of acres belonging to United Fruit Company, in Oriente Province.
May	25	Cuba sends $1 million to Chile, for earthquake relief. Declares that oil purchases from Russia will mean a saving annually of $24 million.
June	10	Twenty million-dollar credit with Czechoslovakia for industrial installations.
June	28	Texaco refinery is "intervened" after its refusal to refine oil, bought from Russia, belonging to the state. Ditto: Esso and Shell.
July	5	Nationalization (intervention) of U.S. industries in Cuba.
July	8	Khrushchev makes his statement that Russian rockets are within reach of America, in case the U.S. should attack Cuba.

July 10 Russia buys the 700,000 tons of sugar which Eisenhower cut from the U.S. quota.

July 15 Visit of Lu Shu Chang, Chinese Vice-Minister of Foreign Commerce.

July 23 Chinese-Cuban commercial treaty.

Aug. 6 Castro announces nationalization of U.S. electric and telephone companies.

Aug. 14 U.S. mines at Moa, Oriente, nationalized.

Sept. 15 Hungary accords Cuba $8 million credit.

Sept. 18 Castro and his delegation arrive in New York (see Appendix 2). The Soviet Premier visits Castro in Harlem's Hotel Theresa. Castro makes his long speech before UN Assembly.

Oct. 13 Nationalization of all the great banks in Cuba.

Oct. 14 Laws of Urban Reform. Castro declares first phase of the revolution fulfilled.

Oct. 21 Guevara begins tour of Communist countries.

Nov. 3 Roa discloses threatening words of President Eisenhower concerning Guantanamo base.

Nov. 10 In Belo Horizonte, Brazilian youth with beards demonstrate solidarity with the Cuban revolution.

Nov. 14 In Matanzas, automatic arms are provided to the new militia. Cuba withdraws from International Bank of Development.

Nov. 15 Castro repeats what he had already said in the speech before the UN Assembly: that the naval base is "a problem of legal right, not force," that Cuba will never use force but will appeal to international law, and that it will give no opportunity to "American imperialism" to provoke aggression against Cuba.

Nov. 16 State Department intervenes against judgment of "mercenaries" who attempted to invade Cuban territory, and Cuba rejects the interference calling the State Department note "disrespectful and insolent."

Nov. 22 Cuban government announces that in 1961 Cuban production of potatoes, beans, poultry, eggs, corn and cotton "will have quintupled." And declares that armed regiments of militia are ready, in case of an invasion.

Nov. 27 Two hundred thousand unemployed peasants, it is announced, will have work; and Cuba will compete with countries that have enhanced their sugar production in order to take up the relinquished sugar quota.

Nov. 30 Cuba and Red China sign a trade treaty, and China grants Cuba $60 million credit without interest and purchase and purchases a million tons of sugar.

More bombings from the air. A mutual tourist accord is reached between Cuba and the Soviet Union. Exchange of 200 students between the two countries, to study technological and agricultural methods.

Dec. 9 George Hess, Canadian Minister of Commerce, announces—against U.S. pressure—that Canada will multiply its trade relations with Cuba.

Dec. 11 John Dieffenbaker, Canadian Premier, in direct reply to U.S. suggestions, declares "Canada's right to trade with whomever it deems proper."

Dec. 19 Moscow announces that if U.S. buys no more Cuban sugar, the Soviets are ready to purchase 2.7 million tons.

Dec. 20 Guevara, from Russia, announces that 100 factories complete are to be shipped to Cuba.

Dec. 22 Czechoslovakia announces a further loan of $20 million, totaling $40 million.

Armando Hart, Minister of Education, names 1961 "Year of Education" and announces that 40,000 classrooms have been opened in new schools.

Poland also grants a credit to Cuba of $20 millions. Secretary-General of Cuba's trade unions declares that the national output of sugar will be 6 million tons, a figure never before attained, representing an income of $358 million. Construction of schools, low-cost dwellings, and cost of the retired and pensioned, will account for $235 million.

1961

The annual budget will come to $1,435 millions.

Jan.   1   A Chinese scientific mission, headed by Kuo Mo Jo, vice-president of China's Academy of Science, visits Cuba.

Jan.   2   The second anniversary of Cuba's independence is celebrated with a parade in Havana's Plaza Civica: a martial demonstration. The army and militia of youth file past with tanks, light and heavy, and with antitank and antiaerial guns. In Matanzas, 500 property titles are handed over to peasants of the province. On the same day Castro informs the U.S. that within 48 hours the American Embassy in Havana must be reduced (from over 100 members) to the same number of officials as employed in the Washington Embassy of Cuba: 11. The U.S. replies to this summary demand by breaking off diplomatic relations with the Castro government. (The reason given by Cuba for the radical reduction of personnel in the U.S. Embassy is that it has become "a hotbed of counter-Castro espionage" and of contact with subversive elements.) Transfer of property titles proceeds by the hundreds in all the provinces of Cuba.

Jan.   7   *Milicianos* in the Escambray Mountains around Trinidad find quantities of American munitions dropped from planes coming from the north, to have been picked up by subversives.

Jan. 11   The Supreme Council of the Urban Reform will apply $35 million for the construction of new dwellings.

Jan. 21   Six complete new factories arrive, from Yugoslavia.

Jan. 23   The workers of various sectors constitute "battalions of voluntary labor" to complete the sugar harvest.

Jan. 27 Half a million students and teachers are mobilized in a campaign to abolish illiteracy throughout the island during 1961.

Feb. 10 The National Federation of Workers, through Conrado Becquer, announces that 112,000 workers in Havana have been organized to speed the cutting of the cane.

Feb. 23 A four-year plan announced by Guevara, beginning 1962, to bring about economic reforms.

Feb. 24 Guevara, the new Minister of Industry, sets up the first systematized economic plan. He declares that in the next five years a billion dollars will be invested in new industries.

Feb. 28 A note is sent to the Hispano-American states, particularizing evidence of plans of U.S. aggression.

Apr. 3 The State Department issues a pamphlet branding the Castro regime as "Communist," and virtually declaring war against it.

Apr. 17 Cuba is invaded by anti-Castro forces. President Kennedy, Adlai Stevenson, Ambassador to UN, deny American participation of any kind. But their lies are cynically admitted, when the coup fails. It becomes known throughout the world that the U.S. Central Intelligence Agency financed, equipped and fully prepared the invasion, with the President in close touch every moment. The prophetic warnings of Chancellor Roa at the UN and the Organization of American States are fully substantiated.

Apr. 28 Fidel Castro discusses their guilt with hundreds of the captured invaders, and promises them to plead for clemency to the Cuban people.

May 1 Castro again offers to discuss mutual problems with the U.S. as between sovereign nations. The U.S. refuses, as it had done on other occasions, including the offer of its good services by Brazil.

May   1   At May Day celebrations, Castro declares that Cuba
            has created the first socialist republic in the Western
            Hemisphere. This is universally interpreted by the
            American press as Cuba's admission that it has
            "wholly entered the bloc of Communist Peoples' Re-
            publics."

Appendix 2
Castro's Lodgings in New York

ON Sunday, September 18, 1960, Fidel Castro arrived in New York as head of the Cuban mission to the General Assembly of the United Nations. For a week its permanent members, Raul Primelles, Manuel Bisbe and Raul Roa Kouri, son of the Chancellor, and their wives had been busy seeking hotel quarters for Castro and his staff, which included at least one Negro. They had not succeeded. The hotels in the East 42nd Street neighborhood, near the UN, informed them that they had no available rooms. Finally the Hotel Shelburne consented to lodge them. This was on the Thursday before Castro's arrival. Later on Friday, the proprietor, perhaps disturbed by the hostile press (one New York daily was to call Cuba's mission "gangsters" in its first page headline) raised the charge for his rooms and demanded a $10,000 bond against possible damage. It was difficult on Saturday to find a broker. But $5,000 cash was procured with the assurance of the balance, in cash or bond, on Monday. When he arrived on Sunday, Castro learned of the $10,000 demand. It angered him. He learned of the refusal of the other hotels, and of the offer of the Hotel Theresa, on 125th Street in the heart of Harlem's Negro ghetto. But the Cuban security police had not approved the Theresa, which they judged too far from the UN for safety. Castro led his group out of the Shelburne to tell his story to the Secretary-General of the UN. Meantime, there were hurried exchanges between the Secretariat and the State Department. The Commodore reversed its previous refusal and offered to house the Cubans gratis. Mr. Spatz of the Shelburne begged Dr. Castro to come back and forget the bond. It was too late. Castro and his delegation went to the Theresa.

Appendix 3
The New Gambling Laws

AT times the new laws display a knowledge wiser than cunning. For example: Gambling has been rampant in Cuba since the conquistadors gambled for gold with death. Attempts to abolish it have been frequent—and in vain. Carlos I tried it; Carlos III in 1771 made it unlawful throughout his kingdoms. From the time of the republic, the lottery has been a chief form of popular demoralization and administrative corruption. Law 86 (February 17, 1959) "totally and definitively suppresses the National Lottery of Cuba." This is traditional; what follows is not.

For lottery tickets, bonds are substituted, each with a serial number. "Weekly drawings will be held among the purchasers of these bonds" (issued by the National Institute for Savings and Housing). "A grand prize of $100,000 plus 1,000 prizes of $100. will be paid out. Those who purchase bonds and do not win any prizes may recover the value of the bonds in accordance with a scale, which ranges from 40% of the value of the bonds if held less than one year to 110% if held more than five years. After a period of five years, the bond, if not cashed, earns 3% annually; after seven years it earns 4% annually."

The old gambling passion of the people hoping to get "something for nothing" in a land where immemorially honest labor has been cheated by parasites and exploiters, is thus re-channeled into a legitimate means of gain with *the role of chance* still present.

Appendix 4
The Cooperatives and Syndicalism

MORE serious than most of the intellectuals' attacks on Cuba is the accusation that Castro has betrayed the excellent 1940 Constitution. In the early days, they say, he promised land to the individual peasant and had very little to say about co-operatives, except in the sense of collective ownership of equipment too expensive to be individually financed. According to this school (typical is Theodore Draper in *Castro's Cuba: A Revolution Betrayed*), Castro switched to the Communists, forgot the freedom of the 1940 law he had promised to restore, and began to imitate the state farms of the Soviet Union in which the individual peasant has as little liberty as in a labor camp.

Whatever the condition of the Russian or Chinese peasant, this gloom is a little previous for Cuba. The cooperative farms and industries of Cuba could well become nuclei of a radical syndicalism developed from the tradition of anarcho-syndicalism which has long appealed to the Spanish and Hispanic worker. Far more than the crude *kholkhoz* within communism, libertarianism might flourish in Cuba within a revised syndicalism. The Draper kind of critic (who reveals in his pamphlet not the faintest firsthand contact with Cuba's people or Cuba's leaders) reckons without the Cuban peasant. The Hispanic record of personal freedom even within the carapace of Church, is very different from the Russian or Chinese. The critic makes unjustified analogies between the man on the Chinese communal farm, the Soviet farmer and the still uncrystalized cooperative of Cuba. It is a little early for such gloom. (I was more reminded in Cuba of the communes of Israel than of those in Russia and China.)

It is true, there is a leveling and regimenting process going on throughout the world: this is the first and uncritical consequence of the machine, in the absence of recognition and development of the person. This danger of regimentation exists in Cuba—and on the farms of Iowa; in Cuba—and on the assembly lines of Detroit. Also it exists in Russia and in China. The notion that this peril is a peculiar Cuban condition due to the invasion of Communist politics is nonsense.

The farm program of INRA did not betray the 1940 Constitution; it went beyond it, as the exigencies of the revolution developed. Castro proceeds, not by a priori theory but from act to act. This is why it is permissible to see in the Cuban cooperatives of every kind a *potential* integration along syndicalist lines. The peril in Cuba must also be seen, and faced, as part of a world condition.

Bibliography   A Personal Selection

This record of books I have read or at least consulted is, I believe, a reasonable selection from the library of books on Cuba or on some aspect of Cuba. But it is far from exhaustive. And it scarcely touches the literature of Cuba, which is prolific and varied. There are fewer Cubans than there are New Yorkers. But a dimension of each Cuban is his fabulously fertile island. This has influenced Cuban novelists, essayists and poets, as it has had effect on the Cuban dance and on Cuban music, both folk and avant-garde. But the focus of this book has been, inevitably, the nation's birth in terms of revolution. Therefore, I have drawn less on literary and aesthetic voices in this cultural portrait than in my other cultural subjects, whose hour of "posing" for portraiture was a quieter one.

One warning to the venturous reader. If he tackles the historians— as he must to place what Cuba was and what it is—he will frequently feel, even with the most scholarly, that he is listening to a debate or a trial in which the chronicler becomes advocate and defender and the United States, including its historians, becomes an ever-present enemy. The Cubans seem to be incapable of objectivity in their accounts of Cuba. Why this has been, I hope the reader of this book will somewhat understand. It is history itself that has put Cuba's historians on the defensive. Let the reader recall what happened at the Battle of Santiago as contrasted with American accounts. Or let him remember how in the popular American mind the honor of discovering the cause of yellow fever was spirited away from Cuban Dr. Carlos Finlay, the true revealer, and wrongly given to the heroic team of Dr. Walter Reed, who verified Finlay's exposition and made it official.

Books in English

A Treaty of Peace between the United States and Spain. 1899.
CARLETON BEALS. *The Crime of Cuba.* 1933.
RAY BRENNAN. *Castro, Cuba and Justice.* 1959.
FRENCH ENSOR CHADWICK. *Relations of the United States and Spain.* 2 vols.

CHARLES E. CHAPMAN. *A History of the Cuban Republic.*
RICHARD HARDING DAVIS. *Cuba in Wartime.* 1897.
———. *The Cuban and Porto Rican Campaigns.* 1898.
CARLOS E. FINLAY, et al. *Carlos Finlay and Yellow Fever.* 1940.
C. H. HARRINGI. *Spanish Empire in America.*
M. HERSKOVITS. *Myth of the Negro Past.* 1940.
HOWARD C. HILL. *Roosevelt and the Caribbean.* 1927.
LEO HUBERMAN AND PAUL SWEEZY. *Cuba, Anatomy of a Revolution.* 1960.
A. HUMBOLDT. *A Political Essay on the Island of Cuba.*
LELAND H. JENKS. *Our Cuban Colony.* 1928.
C. L. JONES, et al. *United States and the Caribbean.* 1929.
CORLISS LAMONT. *Our Crime in Cuba.*
MARGARET LEECH. *In the Days of McKinley.* 1959.
HENRY CABOT LODGE. *The War with Spain.* 1899.
JOHN MASEFIELD. *On the Spanish Main.* (A history of pirates.)
WALTER MILLIS. *The Martial Spirit.* (Study of our war with Spain.)
C. WRIGHT MILLS. *Listen, Yankee.* 1960. (The Castro revolution.)
LOWRIE NELSON. *Rural Cuba.* 1950.
ALLAN NEVINS. *Hamilton Fish.* 1936 (The inner history of the Grant Administration.)
J. H. PARRY. *Spanish Theory of Empire in the XVIth Century.*
——— AND P. M. SHERLOCK. *A Short History of the West Indies.*
HOWARD PYLE. *Buccaneers of America.*
ALBERT G. ROBINSON. *Cuba and the Intervention.* 1905.
THEODORE ROOSEVELT-LEONARD WOOD. *Correspondence.*
ELIHU ROOT. *The Military and Colonial Policy of the United States.* 1916.
ALFRED STERNBECK. *Filibusters and Buccaneers.*
ROBERT TABER. *M 26: biography of a revolution.*
ARTHUR E. TANNER. *Tobacco from Grower to Smoker.*
A. HYATT VERRILL. *In the Wake of the Buccaneers.* 1923.
CARL WERNER. *Textbook on Tobacco.* 1914.
G. WOODBURY. *Great Days of Piracy in the West Indies.*
IRENE ALOHA WRIGHT. *Cuba.* 1911.

Books in Spanish

GERMAN ARCINIEGAS. *Biografía del Caribe.* 1945.
LUIS V. BETANCOURT. *Articulos de Costumbres.* 1880.
MANUEL BISBE, et al. *Vida y Pensamiento de Félix Varela.* 1945.
JULIAN DEL CASAL. *Poesias.*
FIDEL CASTRO. *Discursos.*

————. *Cartas del Presidio.*

————. *History Will Absolve Me.* (Trans. 1961.)

JUAN DE DIOS PEREZ. *Figuras Nacionales.*

FRIEDLAENDER. *Historia Economica de Cuba.* 1944.

MAXIMO GOMEZ. *Cartas.*

RAMIRO GUERRA Y SANCHEZ. *Azucar y Ponlación en las Antillas.*

————. *Expansion Territorial de Estados Unidos.* 1935.

————. *Manual de la Historia de Cuba.* 1938.

P. J. GUITERAS. *Historia de la Isla de Cuba hasta.* 3 vols. 1838.

J. M. HEREDIA. *Cartas y Discursos.*

————. *Poesias.*

ALFONSO HERNANDEZ-CATA. *Mitologia de Martí.*

ALVARO DE LA IGLESIA. *Pepe Antonio.* (Cuban 18th-century life and manners.)

ALCIDES IZNAGA. *Poesias.*

EMILIO ROIG DE LEUCHSENRING. *Obras.*

ANTONIO MACEO. *Ideologia Politica, Cartas y Otros Documentos.* 2 vols.

JORGE MANACH. *Historia y Estilo.*

————. *Martí.*

————. *Obras.*

JUAN MARINELLO. *Martí, Escritor Americano.*

————. *Meditación Americana.*

LEVI MARRERO. *Geografia de Cuba.*

JOSE MARTI. *Cantos Familiares.*

————. *Obras Completas.* 1946 (Havana). 2 vols.

R. MARTINEZ ORTIZ. *Cuba, Los Primeros Años de Independencia.* 1921.

ANTONIO NUNEZ JIMENEZ. *Geografia de Cuba.* 1959. 2nd ed.

————. *La Liberación de las Islas.* 1960.

FERNANDO ORTIZ. *Contrapunteo Cubano del Tabaco y el Azucar.*

————. *Decadencia Cubana.*

————. *Obras Completas.*

————. *Historia de una Pelea Cubana contra los Demonios.* 1959.

HERMINIO PORTELL-VILA. *Historia de Cuba, en sus relaciones con Estados Unidos y Espana.* 1920. 3 vols.

————. *Historia de la Guerra de Cuba y Estados Unidas contra España.*

J. A PORTUONDO. *Bosquejo Historia de las Letras Cubanas.* 1960.

FERNANDO PORTUONDO DEL PRADO. *Historia de Cuba.* 1957.

RAUL ROA. *Viento Sur.*

————. *15 Años Despues.*

M. I. M. RODRIGUEZ. *Los Hombres de la Demajagua.* 1951.

JOSE SACO. *Contra la Anexión.*
————. *El Juego y la Vagancia en Cuba.*
B. SOUZA. *Máximo Gómez.*
CARLOS MANUEL TRELLES. *El Progreso* (1902–1905) *y El Retroceso* (1906–1922) *de la Republica Cubana.*
JOSE ENRIQUE VARONA. *De la Colonia a la Republica.*
————. *Obras Completas.*
CARLOS DE VELAZCO. *Estrada Palma* (contribución historica).
L. ZARRAGOITIA LEDESMA. *Maceo.*